24 DECEMBER 1999

MUCH LOVE...

LESLIE AND GERRY

MAZDA
MX-5
MIATA
Renaissance Sportscar

Other Veloce publications -

Colour Family Album Series
Bubblecars & Microcars by Andrea & David Sparrow
Bubblecars & Microcars, More by Andrea & David Sparrow
Citroen 2CV by Andrea & David Sparrow
Citroen DS by Andrea & David Sparrow
Custom VWs: Beetles, Bugs Kitcars & Buggies by Andrea & David Sparrow
Fiat & Abarth 500 & 600 by Andrea & David Sparrow
Lambretta by Andrea & David Sparrow
Mini & Mini Cooper by Andrea & David Sparrow
Motor Scooters by Andrea & David Sparrow
Vespa by Andrea & David Sparrow
VW Beetle by Andrea & David Sparrow
VW Bus, Camper, Van & Pick-up by Andrea & David Sparrow

SpeedPro Series
How to Blueprint & Build a 4-Cylinder Engine Short Block for High Performance
by Des Hammill
How to Build a V8 Engine Short Block for High Performance
by Des Hammill
How to Build & Modify Sportscar/Kitcar Suspension
by Daniel Stapleton
How to Build & Power Tune Weber DCOE & Dellorto DHLA Carburetors
by Des Hammill
How to Build & Power Tune Harley-Davidson Evolution Engines
by Des Hammill
How to Build & Power Tune Distributor-type Ignition Systems by
Des Hammill
How to Build, Modify & Power Tune Cylinder Heads
by Peter Burgess
How to Choose Camshafts & Camshaft Timing for High Performance Engines
by Des Hammill
How to give your MGB V8 Power
by Roger Williams
How to Power Tune Alfa Romeo Twin Cam Engines
by Jim Kartalamakis
How to Power Tune the BMC/BL/Rover 998cc A-Series Engine
by Des Hammill
How to Power Tune the BMC/Rover 1275cc A-Series Engine by Des Hammill
How to Power Tune Ford SOHC 'Pinto' & Sierra Cosworth DOHC Engines
by Des Hammill
How to Power Tune the MGB 4-Cylinder Engine by Peter Burgess
How to Power Tune the MG Midget & Austin-Healey Sprite
by Daniel Stapleton

General
Alfa Romeo Owner's Bible by Pat Braden
Alfa Romeo Modello 8C 2300 by Angela Cherrett
Alfa Romeo Giulia Coupe GT & GTA by John Tipler
Bentley Continental, Corniche & Azure 1951-1998 by Martin Bennett
British Cars, The Complete Catalogue of 1895-1975
by Culshaw & Horrobin
British Trailer Caravans 1919-1959 by Andrew Jenkinson
Bugatti 46/50 - The Big Bugattis by Barrie Price
Bugatti 57 - The Last French Bugatti by Barrie Price
Chrysler 300 - America's Most Powerful Car by Robert Ackerson
Cobra - The Real Thing! by Trevor Legate
Cortina - Ford's Best Seller by Graham Robson
Daimler SP250 'Dart' by Brian Long
Datsun Z Fairlady to 280Z by Brian Long
Fiat & Abarth 124 Spider & Coupe by John Tipler
Fiat & Abarth 500 & 600 New Edition by Malcolm Bobbitt
Ford F100/F150 Pick-up by Robert Ackerson
Grand Prix & F1 Car, Evolution of the by Simon Read
Jim Redman - Six Times World Motorcycle Champion by Jim Redman
Lea-Francis Story, The by Barrie Price
Lola - The Illustrated History (1957-1977)
by John Starkey
Lola T70 - The Racing History & Individual Chassis Record New Edition
by John Starkey
Making MGs by John Price Williams
Mazda MX5/Miata Enthusiast's Workshop Manual (1.6 models)
by Rod Grainger & Pete Shoemark
MGA by John Price Williams
Mini Cooper - The Real Thing! by John Tipler
Nuvolari: When Nuvolari Raced ... by Valerio Moretti
Porsche 356 by Brian Long
Porsche 911R, RS & RSR New Edition by John Starkey
Porsche 914 & 914-6 by Brian Long
Prince & I (enlarged/revised paperback) by Princess Ceril Birabongse
Rolls-Royce Silver Shadow/Bentley T Series Corniche & Camargue
by Malcolm Bobbitt
Rolls-Royce Silver Wraith, Dawn & Cloud/Bentley MkVI, R & S Series
by Martyn Nutland
Singer Story: Cars, Commercial Vehicles, Bicycles & Motorcycles by Kevin Atkinson
Triumph TR6 by William Kimberley
Triumph Motorcycles & the Meriden Factory by Hughie Hancox
Volkswagen Karmann Ghia by Malcolm Bobbitt
VW Bus, Camper, Van, Pickup (paperback) by Malcolm Bobbitt
Works Rally Mechanic: Tales of the BMC/BL Works Rally Department 1955-1979
by Brian Moylan

First published in 1998 by Veloce Publishing Plc., 33, Trinity Street, Dorchester DT1 1TT, England. Fax: 01305 268864. E-mail: veloce@veloce.co.uk

Readers with ideas for automotive books, or books on other transport or related hobby subjects, are invited to write to Veloce Publishing at the above address.

British Library Cataloguing in Publication Data - A catalogue record for this book is available from the British Library.

Typesetting (Palatino), design and page make-up all by Veloce on AppleMac.

Printed in Hong Kong.

MAZDA
MX-5
MIATA

Renaissance Sportscar

BRIAN LONG

VELOCE PUBLISHING PLC
PUBLISHERS OF FINE AUTOMOTIVE BOOKS

Intro

When the Mazda MX-5 was launched in 1989, it took the world by storm. Journalists from all corners ran out of superlatives - nothing had impressed as much since the appearance of the Datsun 240Z. Mazda introduced its inexpensive convertible - which had all the fun of older machines without the hassle - at just the right time, As many said at the time, Mazda had reinvented the sportscar.

Before long, the MX-5 (also known as the Miata and Eunos Roadster depending on the market) had acquired a reputation which was the envy of the motor industry. The team in Hiroshima was not prepared to rest on its laurels, though, and brought out special versions and a whole series of stunning prototypes. By the end of 1997 the number of examples built was heading towards 450,000 and a mini-industry for aftermarket parts had grown up around the vehicle in virtually every country in which it was sold.

At the 1997 Tokyo Show, Mazda unveiled the second generation MX-5, which went into production in 1998. With looks similar to its predecessor, it incorporated a whole host of improvements and, despite some new competition from MG and a string of other manufacturers, seems set to keep the MX-5 the most popular sportscar currently on the market.

MIATA MX-5 EUNOS

Contents

Preface & Thanks

I have to admit that I didn't become a fan of Mazda until quite recently. In 1991, me and my great friend Simon Pickford travelled to Le Mans in his ageing Daimler SP250 to see our beloved Jaguars thrash the opposition as they had the previous year.

At Le Mans we commented on the glorious exhaust note of a striking green and orange machine that kept bombing around, lap after lap, but never gave it much attention. However, the Big Cats were beaten and at the end of the 24 hours, it was this car - a Mazda - which was declared the winner. From that moment on I had to respect the Mazda marque as it had proved itself in the world's toughest form of competition.

Shortly afterwards I met Miho, the Japanese girl who became my wife, and began to spend a lot of time in Japan. This sparked off a real interest in the Japanese motor industry, with Toyota and Nissan sportscars becoming a pet subject. We also visited a number of Mazda tuners and I fell for the rotary-engined RX-7 - a fast and complex Grand Tourer: it was my kind of car.

When Rod Grainger of Veloce Publishing asked me if I would write the history of the MX-5, I must say I had my doubts. Having a 1968 Alfa Romeo 1750 Spider Veloce in my garage meant the MX-5 was a car that had never really appealed to me. Because of my admiration for the RX-7, however, I took on the project, hoping in the back of my mind that if I did the MX-5 book first, maybe Rod would ask me to do a volume on the RX-7 later.

My original neutral attitude has helped, for as I started my research in the autumn of 1997, I was able to see how thorough Mazda had been, and the real enthusiasm behind the concept, without getting carried away by the myth and hysteria that seem to surround all cult cars.

Personally, I hate to read a book written by someone who obviously loves the car he or she is writing about, for they are rarely able to find or see faults, or even want to look for them in the first place. However, I have to admit even from my standpoint, that I didn't find many. Originally dismissing the MX-5 as too contrived, too clinical, I now have a great deal of respect for the vehicle and the people behind it, and can see why the MX-5 has fans all over the world.

A book is never the work of just one person though. Firstly, I must thank my wife for hour upon hour of translation work and subsequent marathon sessions at the typewriter. Without Miho, the book would be missing the Japanese angle almost completely, and the importance of the home market should never be over-looked.

At Mazda in Japan I would like to acknowledge the help of Tamotsu Maeda and Kensaku Terasaki, and reserve a special thank you for Mayumi Handa - by now, she must dread every fax that comes in from abroad! Having pestered so many of the staff, including Shunji Tanaka and Koichi Hayashi, I sincerely hope that the team in Japan is pleased with the results.

I would also like to thank Mazda in America, particularly Brian Betz and Ellen Clark, Takahiro Tokura of Mazdaspeed, Mazda UK and Bill Livingstone and Alan Beasley of IAD. In addition, many thanks to the various companies which supplied material, such as VeilSide, KG Works, Moss, and so on, plus the many shops that provided me with old brochures.

Behind the scenes, Michitake Isobe (a fellow author and translator), was a great help, as was another friend of ours, Sachiko 'Miko' Miyoshi. There was also Kenji Kikuchi of Nigensha (*Car Graphic*) and Ian Robertson - a Sales Executive at Coventry Mazda and a true MX-5 enthusiast who put up with my many requests.

Paul Grogan of the MX-5 Owners Club was kind enough to help with historical material and read the proof for me, and Peter Hunter - as usual - was a mine of information on all things Japanese.

Brian Long
Coventry
England

A Brief History of Mazda

The history of the Japanese motor industry is a complex one which has been moulded and shaped by government decisions taken in the early-1930s and the reconstruction of Japan following the Second World War.

Mazda's origins date back to January 1920 when the Toyo Cork Kogyo Company Ltd was founded by Jujiro Matsuda. As the name implies, the Hiroshima-based firm initially concerned itself with cork products but the following year Matsuda decided to move into manufacturing machinery.

Jujiro Matsuda was born in August 1875, and despite being brought up in the fishing trade, developed an early interest in metalworking. By the age of 19, he had his own business although it was destined to fail. After various other enterprises, Matsuda eventually decided to move into the supply of cork, as the First World War had stopped exports from Europe and left Japan in short supply. When Europe started to export again, Matsuda guided the company back into light industry.

The car was not yet a popular means of transport for the Japanese at that time. In the early 1920s there were still fewer than 15,000 vehicles in the country, so motor car production was not considered commercially viable. However, a

Jujiro Matsuda - entrepreneur and founder of the Mazda marque.

The first vehicle to bear the Mazda name was this three-wheeled truck. Commercials of this type were built throughout the 1930s, and were revived again shortly after the Second World War.

few two-wheeled machines were built following the devastating Kanto Earthquake of 1923. After the disaster trucks and buses were imported from the United States to get Japan mobile again. Most of the population was centred around the Tokyo Bay (Kanto) area, and the earthquake had totally destroyed thousands of buildings and most of the communications in Tokyo and Yokohama. Matsuda's Hiroshima-based concern on the other side of the country was not affected, and did its best to ease transport problems by building small two-stroke motorcycles.

Although the company still dealt in cork - this part of the business wasn't sold off until 1944 - light industry became increasingly important. In line with this gradual shift of emphasis, in July 1927 the company was renamed the Toyo Kogyo Co. Ltd (which roughly translates as the Orient Industry Company).

The Mazda Marque

Production of Toyo machine tools began in 1929, but by 1930 thoughts were already turning towards motor vehicles. Design work was initiated on a three-wheeled truck (the 482cc Mazda DA), which entered production in October 1931.

As an aside, there is an interesting story behind the choice of the Mazda name. In Persian mythology, the 'lord of light and wisdom' was called Ahura Mazdah. The Mazdah title sounded good in almost any language and had an ideal meaning, with the added bonus of the founder's family name being

Matsuda. Japanese pronunciation makes this sound very like Mazdah. Subsequently, the letter 'h' was dropped, and the Mazda marque was born.

The DA was a great success, and within a few months of production starting Toyo Kogyo began exporting the three-wheeled Mazda to Manchuria - an area of China occupied by Japan. Toyo Kogyo continued to develop the three-wheeler - giving it a larger engine - and also moved into the production of gauge blocks and machine drills.

The company's capital increased no less than four times during 1934, and the factory - based in the Fuchu area of Hiroshima - was expanded. However, military considerations caused the government to pass the 1936 Motorcar Manufacturing Enterprise Law. Although only Nissan, Toyota and Isuzu complied with the new law at the time, it effectively ended the activities of

the foreign car companies: Ford and General Motors cut back production and then closed their factories in Japan during 1937. Toyo Kogyo was forced to make munitions for the Army, but a few three-wheelers continued to leave the factory, despite the new Enterprise Law being in force. By 1940, Mazda had built a small prototype coupé; however, before it could be developed further, production switched completely to armaments in the build-up to the Pacific War.

After the attack on Pearl Harbour, America declared war on Japan, but no-one could have foreseen the dreadful events that would follow. On 6 August 1945, Hiroshima became a scene of complete devastation. A broadcast from Tokyo Radio stated: 'Most of Hiroshima no longer exists. The impact of the bomb was so terrific that practically all living things, human and animal, were literally seared to death by the tremendous

Mazda's three-wheeler took on a more substantial appearance with the arrival of the CT series in 1950. This is the 1953 CTA. Three-wheelers continued well into the 1960s. The T2000 of 1962 vintage had a load-carrying capacity of two tons.

heat and pressure engendered by the blast.'

Despite this, the Toyo Kogyo factory was just far enough away from the centre of the blast to escape heavy damage. Sadly though, the bomb dropped by *Enola Gay* claimed 78,000 lives and injured almost as many again. The end of the Second World War came later that month, but it would take many years to restore some kind of normality to the lives of those - on all sides - who suffered as a result of the conflict.

Postwar growth

Toyo Kogyo resumed production of its Mazda three-wheelers at the end of 1945. In three years the capital of the company doubled and up to 200 vehicles were being built each week. Larger commercials were announced in 1950, but the company did not move into the passenger car business for another decade.

Various laws were passed to help the Japanese motor industry and gradually it found its feet. Production rose steadily, new roads were built and Tokyo streets began to fill with Japanese cars rather than ageing imported models. Steel and components could now be produced in Japan as most factories had been returned to their original owners by the Occupational Forces, and there was less need to buy from foreign countries.

Commercial vehicles continued to sustain the Hiroshima concern, but in April 1960 the company introduced its first car - the R360 Coupé. It went on sale in May with an air-cooled, V-twin, rear-mounted engine. Although the 356cc unit developed only 16bhp, it could be purchased with either manual or automatic transmission and was capable of 56mph. It sold exceptionally well - over 20,000 were built in the first year.

After the war a number of Japanese manufacturers had taken the opportunity of entering into technical co-operation agreements with companies in the West. Toyo Kogyo was quite late in taking this up, but eventually, in November 1961, signed a deal with NSU of Germany.

NSU held the rights to the Wankel rotary engine, an advanced piece of engineering. Mazda must have calculated that it would be able to catch up with the likes of Nissan and Toyota by being the first vehicle builder in Japan to acquire this technology. Over the next five years, whilst the rotary engine was being developed, Toyo Kogyo introduced a number of new Mazda cars - the Carol P360 and P600, the first generation of Familia models and the Luce 1500. (The coachwork on the Luce 1500 was designed by the famous Italian styling house, Bertone, and Giugiaro has been credited with the design.)

In the meantime, cumulative production (commercial vehicles and cars added together) reached one million units in March 1963, and two years later the Miyoshi Proving Ground was completed. By this time Toyo Kogyo was the third largest car producer in Japan, continually expanding its operations at a staggering rate. In 1966 a new passenger car plant opened in Hiroshima, and in the following year, full-scale exports for the European market began.

The Cosmo Sports 110S

Toyo Kogyo - under the leadership of Jujiro Matsuda's son, Tsuneji, since 1951 - was certainly a forward-thinking organisation. At the 1964 Tokyo Show held at Harumi, the Mazda Cosmo Sports 110S made its debut. Powered by the company's first Wankel engine, it was extremely advanced and had given the Rotary Engine Development Division quite a few teething troubles in the early days. It underwent an extraordinary period of development before going on sale to the public, with a total of sixty pre-production models being road tested. Consequently, the Mazda Cosmo did not

The first Mazda car was the R360 Coupé of mid-1960 which had a tiny air-cooled V-twin engine. Over 20,000 examples were sold in the first year of production.

The rotary-engined Cosmo Sports 110S of 1967. Around 350 of these early models were built before the Cosmo underwent a minor facelift in mid-1968. Its high price tag limited total sales to just over 1500 units over a run covering six years.

The home-market Savanna GT of 1972, better known abroad as the RX-3. Like the RX-2 (which was also rotary-engined), it came as an attractive coupé (as seen here) or with four-door saloon bodywork. An estate version augmented the RX-3 range.

The car you've waited 85 years for.

A British advertisement dating from March 1970 for the Mazda R100 Coupé, which was known in Japan as the Familia Rotary Coupé. It was also sold in the United States but acquired round headlights for that market. Its elegant lines were bettered only by the contemporary Luce Rotary Coupé - a pillarless two-door model based on the Luce 1500 saloon.

go on sale until May 1967, by which time the engineers had perfected the power unit. Selling at 1,580,000 yen, it was very costly (only the Toyota 2000GT was more expensive in the sportscar sector of the Japanese market), and this was reflected in a total run, from 1967 to 1972, of just 1519 units.

In October 1969 the Japan Automatic Transmission Company (JATCO) was formed. This was a joint venture between Toyo Kogyo,

Ford and Nissan for the manufacture of automatic gearboxes. As the rotary engine had passed Federal tests that year, exports to the United States began shortly afterwards, and the first cars - with rotary and more conventional engines in the line-up - arrived there in the spring of 1970. Within a year, Mazda dealerships were selling the cars before they had time even to unload them from the transporters.

On the death of Tsuneji Matsuda in November 1970, the reins were passed to his son, Kohei, the third generation of the Matsuda family to head the company. There was a whole string of important introductions during the early-1970s: the Mazda Capella (RX-2) was followed by the Savanna (RX-3) and, in 1972, the Luce (RX-4) made its debut. Mazda cars were now beginning to outsell trucks on a regular basis. By the end of 1972, cumulative production had reached a staggering five-million units, and the Mazda Technical Centre had been established in Irvine, California.

The oil crisis held up a

An official photograph of the 1973 RX-4 Coupé from the UK concessionaires. The era known as the 'Sporting Forties' (1965-74 in Japanese Emperor years) spawned a number of exciting vehicles from the 'Land of the Rising Sun.'

number of interesting projects such as the X020G 2+2 coupé. Rotary engines, some rated up to 200bhp, were being prepared, but the timing was not right and sales of rotary-engined cars as a whole began to suffer as fuel economy became the overriding consideration with new car buyers. As a result, Toyo Kogyo soon ran into financial troubles and had to turn to the Sumitomo Bank for help to keep the company afloat. This backing was eventually forthcoming but the Matsuda family lost some of its power in the process.

The RX-7 Savanna

1977 saw the introduction of the Familia (the original GLC/323), which helped combat the downturn in Mazda sales, but it was the car that was launched in 1978 that was important to sportscar enthusiasts.

Things were starting to happen in Japan as far as the sportscar world was concerned. Nissan had been building the

highly-successful Fairlady Z since late-1969, but during 1978 it took a distinct move upmarket. Mazda had launched the RX-7 (known in Japan as the Savanna) in March 1978, and in effect this took the market position of the old Fairlady Z as a cheap but competent sportscar, selling for 1,440,000 yen.

As Kohei Matsuda said in late-1977: 'A two-seater sportscar may well represent the ultimate design compliment for the rotary engine.' He was absolutely right: the Mazda marque had already acquired a reputation among motorsport enthusiasts for its sporting machines, but the rotary-engined RX-7 established the Japanese car maker in all corners of the world, and signalled a turnaround in the fortunes of the Wankel power unit.

Of course, the RX-7 was admired on the home market as well, and received the "Japanese Car of the Year" award. However, by the time it was officially put on sale, Yoshiki Yamasaki had become

the first head of the company who was not a member of the Matsuda family.

Revival, and links with Ford

Sales started to pick up again after introduction of the conventionally powered Familia family car and the immensely popular RX-7. Cumulative production reached ten million vehicles in 1979, but in November that year Ford acquired a 24.5 per cent equity stake in Mazda. Within three years, Mazda was marketing Ford-brand vehicles through its Autorama sales channel in Japan. This arrangement actually worked both ways, as a number of Mazdas (such as the B-series pick-up) had been badged as Fords in the States, and vehicles were later developed jointly on both sides of the Pacific.

In the meantime, 1980 brought with it the introduction of the front-wheel drive Mazda Familia (also known as the GLC or 323, depending on the market). The Familia was presented with the coveted 1980-1981 "Japanese Car of the Year" award, and over one million had been produced by 1982.

As a matter of interest, Japanese manufacturers built seven million vehicles between them during 1980, helping Japan to become the world's number one car-producing country. Mazda (North America) Inc. - better known as MANA - was established during 1981 and became a key organisation in the initial stages of the MX-5's development. Despite unfavourable exchange rates, almost 170,000 Mazdas were sold in the States that year: the GLC became a best-seller in the economy sector, while the facelifted RX-7 appealed to sportscar enthusiasts.

1982 saw the introduction of the fwd Mazda Capella (or 626). It immediately received the 1982-83 "Japanese Car of the Year" title in its native country, was named *Motor Trend* magazine's 1983 "Import Car of the Year" and also received a large number of other prestigious accolades overseas. Sales in America continued to climb as the appeal of the Mazda range widened.

Toyo Kogyo entered into an 8 per cent capital tie-up with Kia Motors in 1983, and cumulative production reached 15 million units. From a very small beginning, the Mazda marque had grown at great speed and had a range of vehicles which could compete in all markets, challenging established car manufacturers throughout the world. However, Toyo Kogyo was not yet satisfied with its achievements ...

The Familia, known as the GLC in America and the 323 elsewhere. Although not the most interesting Mazda ever built, its conventional fuel-efficient engine helped Toyo Kogyo to survive an uncertain period in its history. This American advert dates from early 1978.

The RX-7 was an instant hit in Britain. Tony Dron won his class in one in the BTCC in 1979, and Win Percy took the Championship outright with the RX-7 in 1980 and 1981. Tom Walkinshaw was another successful Mazda racer, and these are TWR-modified road cars from 1981. From left to right: the front-wheel-drive 323, the 626 Coupé and the RX-7 Turbo.

The Mazda RX-7, seen here in home-market limited form at the time of its launch, was hugely popular in America, despite the fuel crisis and unfavourable exchange rates. An excellent competition record in the United States probably helped convince enthusiasts and the car also received a number of awards in Japan.

The Toyo Kogyo business was renamed the Mazda Motor Corporation on 1 May 1984, with 61-year-old Kenichi Yamamoto elected President. Yamamoto had been with Toyo Kogyo for many years and had been the company's Chief Engineer since January 1978.

Yamamoto had seen a vast number of changes along the way. On the technological front he was responsible for designing three-wheeled Mazda trucks shortly after the war, and was heavily involved with the R360 and its descendants; he was also one of the key people behind the development of the Mazda rotary engine. He'd witnessed the growth of the company to leading car manufacturer, and behind all of his achievements in the field of engineering was a dedicated enthusiasm for his work - an important factor that would have a bearing on the future.

MANA

Mazda (North America) Inc. (MANA) had a Product Planning & Research (PP&R) arm, and this was managed by Shigenori Fukuda. The idea behind this department was that its findings should give Mazda a much better feel for the market so that future vehicles could be tailored to suit the tastes of different countries.

One of the first Americans to join the PP&R office was Bob Hall, a true car enthusiast with a background in automotive journalism and British sportscars, and he was keen on the idea of a modern equivalent of the latter. In spring of 1979, Hall was casually asked what he would like to see

Toyo Kogyo building. The question came at the end of a meeting with Kenichi Yamamoto (when Hall was still working as a journalist). Hall suggested that Mazda should make a lightweight sportscar at a price even cheaper than the RX-7's.

On a trip to the Pebble Beach concours event, Hall soon found he was not alone in this idea. Shunji Tanaka, one of the group over from Japan to evaluate the RX-7 in the all-important American market, was asked by Hall what type of car he would like to design next. His reply was 'a lightweight sportscar.' Naturally, this drew an enthusiastic response and Fukuda and Ryo Uchida soon became involved in the conversation as well.

Not long after this, an appraisal entitled *What is a Sportscar to an American?* was sent through to the head office. This was quite a lengthy piece, but the most important paragraphs read as follows: 'Sportscars must have a degree of performance, but more importantly, they must be fun to drive. A low-cost sportscar doesn't need 0.81g lateral acceleration or 0-60 in 8.5 seconds. It has to, as one journalist succinctly put it, "feel faster than it is, but it doesn't have to be fast in absolute terms." Of course, a sportscar mustn't be a sluggard either, so it is a classic example of searching for the happy medium.

'Appearance (particularly one's first impression) and performance are obvious things which make a sportscar, but there are a couple of intangibles, too. Not the least of these is image. If you look back in history, all (not some or most, but all) of the successful sportscars have developed a cult-like following of enthusiasts, a core of people who have an almost maniacal enthusiasm for the particular make and model of car they own - MG or Lotus Elan enthusiasts, for example. Most of these people would never race or rally their car, but they won't buy anything else. This image is essential to a successful sportscar. The MGs all had it - Saab's Sonnet never did. Any TR-series Triumph possessed this element, but try as hard as they could, Sunbeam wasn't ever able to develop such an image for the Alpine.

'There have also been a lot more successful convertible sportscars than coupés, at least in the United States and Canada. The Opel GT, Marcos 1800, Glas 1700 GT, Lancia Montecarlo (Scorpion in America), Simca 1000 and (in later forms) Saab Sonnet were all pretty, but there wasn't a convertible (or a success) among them. Even Targas are not open cars to most sportscar owners. This is not to say that a light sportscar cannot succeed without a convertible [top], but an $8000 convertible among a flock of $9000 - $12,000 coupés and Targas should be as popular as beer at a baseball stadium.'

It was obvious that the people at MANA thought America was in need of an affordable sportscar. At this stage in the proceedings, however, nothing was heard from Hiroshima.

An LWS

A friend of the author's, Yoshihiko Matsuo, chief designer of the original Fairlady Z (240Z) and now a design consultant, gave his definition of a modern sportscar in a recent interview: 'It must be a two-passenger automobile with attractive body styling designed for high-speed, highly responsive driving. The engine must have reserves of power even at high rpm. It should have a manual transmission with a good feel and a fully functional cockpit, and support pleasant high-speed handling. To state it as a category, I would say that sportscars belong somewhere between speciality cars and racing prototypes. Also, I believe, there are two main types of sportscars, one the Lightweight Sportscar and the other the Super Sportscar.'

The Mazda RX-7 wasn't exactly lightweight, but it was nearer the lightweight concept than most. Weighing in at around 1100kg, it was substantially lighter than Nissan's S130 series Fairlady (280ZX), and the recently introduced Z31 models. But the RX-7 was destined to follow the Fairlady in its move upmarket: the P747 would be bigger, faster, heavier and better equipped. In other words, the second-generation RX-7 was going to be a Super Sportscar.

The first-generation RX-7 sold in massive quantities in the United States, just like the original affordable Japanese sportscar of the 1970s, the 240Z. The Toyota Celica was another success story. Of course, exchange rates at the time helped, but these cars were not the flukes some would have you believe; nothing in Japanese business happens by chance. By careful research the Japanese had found the formula: offer excellent value in an attractive, reliable package and it's a licence to print money.

However, with the new RX-7 scheduled for the 1986 Model Year (work had started on it in 1981), this was going to leave a void in the market as far as Japanese manufacturers were concerned. Toyota immediately spotted this niche and tried to fill it with the mid-engined MR2, but in America - the world's biggest sportscar market - it was not as successful as was hoped, probably because Pontiac brought out the Fiero just beforehand. Honda also saw the gap and launched the sporty front-engined, front-wheel drive CRX, but this could never be considered a true sportscar in the great tradition of the S500, S600 and S800 roadsters.

The Mazda marque was flying high in the States at that time, with the RX-7 dominating the IMSA racing scene and the SCCA Pro-Rally series. Kenichi Yamamoto knew that a true LWS - an abbreviation of lightweight sportscar, a term used within the trade in much the same way as MPV (multi-purpose vehicle), and so on - would potentially have the market to itself and further strengthen Mazda's sporting image.

Yamamoto had got the sportscar bug after Hirotaka Tachibana of the Experimental Department and Takaharu Kobayakawa (one of Yamamoto's most respected engineers who had been Chief Engineer on the RX-7 since 1986) - both LWS enthusiasts of the highest order - had encouraged him to take a business trip to

Tokyo via the mountain roads around Hakone in a Triumph Spitfire. After this, he knew that Mazda should try and develop a similar vehicle. Judging by MANA's essay sent to Hiroshima in 1982, it thought the market needed an entry-level sportscar as well.

The Mazda Technical Research Centre in Hiroshima was still in the planning stage (it opened in 1985), so as something of a stop-gap, in November 1983, the company established a programme to allow its designers to think up and develop ideas for vehicles outside their recognised range. This programme was given the bizarre name, "Off-Line, Go, Go."

Managing Director Michinori Yamanouchi hoped that this programme would encourage engineering and design staff to take a fresh approach and, indeed, Off-Line, Go, Go (or OGG) brought about some novel proposals. The subject of this book was one of the projects to be tackled off-line - a lightweight sportscar.

A competition

Once the LWS project had been chosen, there was the matter of which layout to select. It was decided that the three main possibilities: FR (front engine, rear drive) FF (front-wheel-drive) and MR (mid-engined) would be split so that each idea could be developed properly. After some far from subtle hints, the FR layout went to MANA in the States, while the FF and MR cars were assigned to the Tokyo Design Studio in Japan. The resulting designs would then go through two rounds of judging in Hiroshima and a winner declared. Masakatsu Kato, who was behind many of Mazda's concept cars, was

Two of the design drawings submitted by MANA for the ideal lightweight sportscar.

given the task of overseeing the project - code number P729.

Although there were no firm plans for the LWS as yet, Mazda was seriously considering producing a Familia Cabriolet. Mark Jordan, who had joined MANA in January 1983, was put in charge of the project. The son of Chuck Jordan (the head of design at General Motors), he came from talented stock. A car was duly built and the model eventually joined the Mazda line-up.

However, the team at MANA was far more interested in the LWS project. By this time, Fukuda, Jordan, Hall and stylist Masao Yagi (Fukuda's assistant who had been sent to the States from Hiroshima), had already begun working on their ideal open sportscar. Tsutomo Matano joined MANA at the end of 1983 as head of the design section, having worked for GM and BMW and earning an excellent reputation along the way.

Tom Matano wasn't particularly happy with the facilities at MANA when he first moved there, although the LWS project that he took over had great appeal: 'When I joined Mazda, the first project I worked on was the Miata, and I thought this was a good chance for me to really put my emotions and passions together to make a car.'

Having said that it was the Bertone-styled Alfa Romeo Giulia Canguro of 1964 which had inspired him to become a car designer in the first place, Tom's view concerning the background to the project was quite significant: 'I think what we're looking for is the simplicity of the era, say, the Sixties. We want to get back to a

August 1984. The first model from MANA which set the LWS project in motion. Tom Matano said his team had set out 'to recapture the spirit of the British sportscar,' but no-one could have anticipated at the time the huge success of the subsequent production model.

relationship between car and driver that simply brings fun [to the driver]. At a time when British sportscars had all gone ... due to either safety rules or emission rules and so forth, the fun element was really disappearing out of the market. And again, another urge was to provide the type of car that we loved when we were younger ... [We thought] a small sportscar with a convertible [top] has to have a place in the future as it had in the past.'

Shortly after Matano joined the team, a layout engineer by the name of Norman Garrett III signed up for MANA as well. Given that the American LWS would use an FR layout (the one preferred by most traditional sportscar enthusiasts and the MANA team), Garrett decided to use components from the existing Mazda range - an old rwd GLC (323) engine and its associated transmission, and MacPherson struts all-round for the suspension.

Although a fresh approach

could have been used (that was the reason behind the formation of OGG, after all), it was hoped that by using parts which could be easily sourced from within the organisation, the project stood more chance of being accepted.

Meanwhile, two lightweight coupés were being designed in the Tokyo Design Studio - one, a front-wheel-drive model (FF), and the other a mid-engined (MR) vehicle. The FF design had a distinct advantage, as the 323 was moving in this direction and would make an obvious donor car if the design was allowed to progress.

Having been involved with the RX-7, Yoichi Sato was quite keen to produce a car to compete with the Honda CRX, and set about his task with the help of Hideki Suzuki in their small office in the Gotanda district of Tokyo, not far from Haneda airport. Early drawings included a convertible but, eventually, an attractive coupé was settled on. However, the mid-engined vehicle, with its wedge

The Tokyo Design Studio's FF coupé in profile. The drawings based around this layout were perhaps better than the full-sized clay, although the nose was very attractive. A convertible had also been suggested in the early stages of the design process.

The MR design submitted by Sato and Suzuki. An interesting proposal, the overall dimensions were very close to those of the recently-introduced Toyota MR2.

A rear view of the MR model. In fact, the MR layout was always going to struggle, as Maasaki Watanabe had built an experimental mid-engined 323 and dismissed it on NVH (Noise, Vibration and Harshness) grounds.

MANA's Duo 101 in profile.

shape and sharp roofline, was more distinctive. Indeed, when the competitors met for the first round of the contest in April 1984, it was the MR machine that looked the most impressive on paper.

Seconds out, round two ...

When the second round of competition was held in August, the FF design was looking odds-on favourite. The MR design, meanwhile, had an uphill battle on its hands as Watanabe had already built a Familia with the MR layout and declared it unsuitable for production. It had dimensions very close to those of the recently-announced Toyota MR2, and with the Pontiac Fiero also available the mid-engined sportscar market was already probably better catered for than it had been since the 1970s.

The second phase of the competition was to present full-scale clays and through this process the MANA proposal suddenly came alive. Even Sato was impressed, saying 'Their full-size model was a quantum leap from those flat sketches.' The design (which was actually the first clay to be built at the Irvine studio) was christened the "Duo 101" by the staff at MANA - Duo apparently signifying that either a hard- or soft-top could be used.

Fukuda and Hall put forward a whole host of reasons outlining why the FR layout was more suitable in a car of this type, and even put together a video presentation to try and sway the judges' decision. It was a very professional approach which ultimately paid off. The MANA team won and

were therefore destined to play an important part in the early stages of Mazda's LWS project.

A brave decision?

At the time, the decision to go for the convertible may have seemed a brave move, but, in retrospect, there was an obvious gap in the market. The Alfa Romeo Spider was suffering from a lack of investment and ongoing development, and the Fiat Spider, latterly badged as a Pininfarina model, was about to fade from the scene.

There wasn't really much else available, unless one was willing to look at low-volume models, special conversions on existing coupés, or very expensive convertibles. But it wasn't always this way; look in any 1960s American magazine and there will almost certainly be more adverts for open British sportscars than for homegrown products. However, by 1970 British manufacturers had completely lost their stronghold on the American market.

Forthcoming Federal regulations seemed to dictate the end of

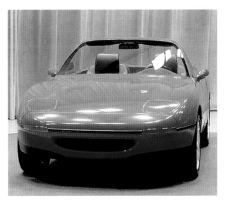

A front view of the FR (Duo 101) model. Note the stylish air intake and small door mirrors.

The attractive Kamm tail of the Duo 101. Neat touches abound, such as the hidden door releases and the fairing on the rear deck.

The Duo 101 with hardtop in place. Shigenori Fukuda can be seen in the middle of the picture, draping his jacket over his shoulder.

the convertible, but it's too easy to cite this as the sole cause of the extinction of the cheap sporty models emanating from UK shores. In fact, a number of reasons contributed and car builders have to accept some blame for poor build quality, archaic specifications and lack of customer care.

Reliability problems were another factor. The author has owned a string of sportscars that would appeal to the enthusiast, so can confirm as well as anyone that the occasional problem is accepted and passed off as thoroughbred temperament. However, after a while it soon becomes wearing and with the introduction of the Datsun Fairlady roadsters (and then the legendary 240Z), many sportscar enthusiasts were converted to Japanese products which not only spent more time on the road instead of in the garage, but also offered exceptional value for money.

This spoilt the Americans, who experienced the qualities of Japanese cars in SCCA racing as well. When the Triumph TR7 became available as a convertible (it was designed as a pure coupé from the start as it was thought soft-top cars would be banned in the US), an American magazine carried out a loyalty survey to see if existing owners would buy another. In stark contrast to cars like the 240Z and RX-7, the results were some of the worst recorded. In Europe, too, although sportscar buyers were a little less receptive to these Oriental impersonators, the Japanese were certainly making inroads.

Japan had not built many convertibles since the war, and most of the early-1980s Japanese convertible cars consisted of coupés converted to cabriolets by third parties. Avatar did this with the first generation RX-7 before Mazda brought out its own convertible on the second generation RX-7. Other notable examples included ASC's work on the Celica, and Richard Straman's 300ZX and cheap little roadster based on the Honda Civic. Interestingly, all of these conversions were carried out in North America.

Looking back, the Datsun DC-3 was probably the first purpose-built Japanese convertible, sold during 1952. Nissan built a few soft-top prototypes before launching the Datsun Fairlady Roadsters. There was also a prototype 240Z drophead, but sadly this failed to make it into production due to proposed Federal regulations.

There was also the Mikasa but very few were sold. Other rarities included the Prince Skyline Sport Convertible and Daihatsu Compagno. Honda built a run of successful roadsters, and Toyota took the roof off a 2000GT for a James Bond movie, but it wasn't until the third generation Celica that Toyota listed a convertible in its line-up. The examples mentioned show that the Japanese had hardly flooded the market with convertibles, the best-selling models having gone out of production over a decade before the 1980s.

The American authorities didn't pass the regulations outlawing the soft-top, but even though the convertible's future seemed assured, surprisingly few manufacturers took the opportunity to build one. It seemed the consensus of opinion was that the convertible market had simply ceased to exist after 1970. Maybe Mazda was right to explore the possibilities and by using the OGG route the company didn't have to commit itself fully until totally satisfied there was still sufficient interest. Although the LWS project was not guaranteed production status at this stage, the team at MANA was convinced it would eventually find its way into showrooms.

IAD

In September 1984, International Automotive Design, better-known as IAD, was asked by Mazda to become involved with the LWS project. IAD was founded by the late John Shute (an ex-GM body engineer and avid collector of MGs) in the early 1970s. Based in Worthing in the South of England, IAD soon had an excellent reputation for developing prototypes and Shute was well-known in the trade.

Mazda wanted its new car to have a British flavour and actually commissioned IAD to build a running prototype based on the Duo 101 and carry out evaluations of a number of British classics. Cars - including the original Lotus Elan - were tested at the MIRA facility in the centre of England and reports compiled.

A fibreglass lookalike open body and makeshift interior were constructed around mechanical components from a selection of Mazda models: the 1.4-litre engine

The completed IAD running prototype built in glassfibre and with a backbone chassis. It was based on the first MANA clay - the second clay had the air intake removed at the front, relocated door handles and different rear lights.

A rear view of the V705. Note the exceptionally large rear screen area and Toyota reference on the number plate - typical British humour.

When the IAD-built V705 prototype arrived in America for its Santa Barbara excursion, the RX-7 wheels were changed for some multi-spoke items that would not give a clue to the car's true identity. Arriving on the back of a car transporter wrapped in a grey cover, the vehicle was made ready for its drive around the local area, but its numberplates from a Mazda distributor soon gave the game away.

and transmission came from a rwd Familia; front suspension and wheels were taken from an early RX-7 and rear suspension was from a Luce (929). The interesting part of the prototype was the use of a backbone chassis designed and built in-house by IAD. Given the code number V705 by Mazda, the car - with its fibreglass body (a feature Kato had insisted on at this early stage), backbone chassis and FR layout - was, in effect, the Japanese equivalent of the original Lotus Elan. The V705 was to be fully-functional and was completed in August 1985 under the direction of Project Manager, Bill Livingstone.

California dreamin'

The enthusiastic team at MANA had done little on the LWS project since it was handed over to IAD, but work had recently started again to enable some subtle design changes to the body, the eventual result being the S-2 clay. In the meantime, on 17 September 1985, Mazda staff from both Japan and America met up in Worthing to view and drive the IAD prototype in England.

On the first day, the car was viewed in the IAD works, but on the second day the group, led by Masakatsu Kato, was taken to the Ministry of Defence test track not too far from IAD, where the V705 was compared on a high-speed loop, a road course and a skid pan with a Fiat X1/9, a Toyota MR2 and the new Reliant Scimitar. Everyone was exceptionally happy with the car. Mark Jordan wrote in his report that IAD 'did an excellent job. After testing the car, it felt very pleasing ...'

The car was scheduled to be shipped back to Japan, but on the orders of Managing Director, Masataka Matsui, newly-appointed head of the Technical Research Centre, it was sent to the USA instead. Matsui wanted to see the new car in its natural environment, which made sense, but it was also very risky because the car could have been seen by someone from the motoring journals. For this reason, somewhere that wasn't too busy had to be chosen and Santa Barbara seemed the ideal place.

In mid-October, Matsui arrived in California to see the new car in the setting it was designed for. MANA had assembled a small group of cars for comparison (an RX-7, a Triumph Spitfire and a Honda convertible by the Straman concern), and took the V705 to Santa Barbara on a car transporter. Anyone remotely interested in cars came to look at the vehicle which wasn't exactly anonymous as it carried Californian plates borrowed from a local distributor.

Unfortunately, whilst testing, the Mazda crew came across a number of journalists also testing cars; the plates gave the game away. Bob Hall, being an ex-writer, explained the situation and somehow managed to get the journalists to agree not to publish any photographs.

In retrospect, Fukuda thought it was a mistake to expose the car so early. Overall, though, it was a highly successful day. Matsui was more than happy with public response at this impromptu 'clinic.' At dinner with the MANA team that evening, Matsui was convinced that the LWS had potential and declared 'I think we should build this car.' More importantly, when he returned to Hiroshima, he gave the LWS project his full support.

Virtual reality

1985 saw the introduction of the all-new fwd Mazda Familia (323) series in Japan, and the second generation Savanna RX-7. The RX-7 was duly named 1986 'Import Car of the Year' by *Motor Trend* magazine.

A number of interesting concept cars appeared as well. Suzuki displayed its R/S1 LWS at the 1985 Tokyo Show; amazingly, despite favourable reaction, this car never made it into production so the way was still clear for Mazda. The Hiroshima marque displayed the MX-03, a four-wheel drive, four-wheel steer coupé designed by Kato, at the same event. With 2+2 seating, it was sportier than the MX-02 of two years earlier (which was quite staid by comparison), but was destined to remain a prototype.

Shigenori Fukuda returned to Japan to take up the post of General Manager of the Design Division. Having been closely involved with the LWS project from its birth, Fukuda was obviously keen to see it through to the end as it was the epitome of his "Romantic Engineering" concept. However, the LWS was still not guaranteed a place in the Mazda showrooms. At the end of the 1980s, Fukuda stated that 'the project was interupted several times.' In fact, Shunji Tanaka feels that had Fukuda not returned to Japan, the LWS might never have seen the light of day.

There were a number of reasons for doubt about the LWS's future. Mazda had already approved its new MPV which, with the benefit of hindsight, was an excellent move (Japan's roads are full of these utility vehicles nowadays), but was also pushing for a car in the Light (or *Kei*) class. The Light Car was a proven winner, and with the limited resources available, many in the company recommended this route be taken and the LWS be suspended.

Fortunately, this immediate problem was overcome via a joint engineering agreement with Suzuki in relation to the K-car - released resources meant Mazda could do the MPV, the K-car (the Carol) *and* the LWS, but the men in the finance department were still not too happy. America was always going to be the main market for an open sportscar, and the value of the yen was making life hard for Japanese exports.

The first major Japanese sportscar success on the US market, the Datsun 240Z, hit the shores of America in 1970. The floating exchange rate system was introduced in 1971 and almost immediately the yen began to strengthen against the dollar. By 1972, 300 yen would buy a dollar instead of the 357 needed at the start of the previous year.

With the oil crisis of 1973, the yen was quoted at 253 per dollar before the dollar recovered dramatically. By the end of the 1970s when Mazda's RX-7 came onto the scene, the rate had dropped to below 200 yen to the dollar and was still moving in the same direction. 1985 had seen the yen moving strongly against the dollar, pushing prices in export markets up to unprecedented levels, which had an obvious effect on sales.

This was not such an easy problem to resolve as the thinking behind the LWS was that it should be cheap enough to tempt people into buying what was, at the end of the day, something of an indulgence.

In January 1985, AutoAlliance International Inc., a 50/50 venture with Ford, was established in Flat Rock, Michigan. Having a manufacturing plant in the States would overcome currency fluctuations (MX-6 production began in September 1987, followed shortly after by the Ford Probe and later the 626), but there were no plans to build the LWS there. Careful design, to keep production costs down, would be the car's saviour.

In the meantime, progress was slow. MANA eventually completed the S-2 clay in December 1985 and the P729 was officially presented to the Mazda Board the following month. Yamamoto was fully behind the LWS idea, saying it had 'a smell of culture.' Managing Director Takashi Kuroda also expressed his support, and for this reason, on 18 January 1986 the P729 was grudgingly given approval. But then there was another, unexpected delay ...

Kato, who had overseen the project since inception, decided to step down from his position as head of P729 and concentrate his

The third and final clay produced by MANA.

efforts on new ideas within the recently-opened Technical Research Centre. Naturally this meant a replacement had to be found. Fortunately, Toshihiko Hirai, previously in charge of the Familia (323), made it known that he would like to be considered for the LWS project. Born in 1935, Hirai was well-respected and had a proven record with the successful 323 range. With his vast engineering experience and a spell in the Service Department, he was declared the ideal man for the job and in February took up with relish his new post as the P729's Chief Engineer.

In the same month, MANA was told it could start on the third and final clay model (the S-3) and work began in earnest in the middle of March. Tom Matano and Koichi Hayashi were responsible for the majority of input, ably supported by Mark Jordan and Wu-Huang Chin.

Matano wanted to develop a family resemblance between the "faces" of the various cars in the Mazda range - a frontal view that would immediately single out the car as a Mazda. Using BMW and

Mercedes-Benz grilles as examples, he went on: 'To us, this is a graphical way of identifying the car. It's great if you have a [long] heritage, and so forth, that establishes you in such a way, but at this point in Mazda's development we wanted to upgrade our image ... To achieve that, we wanted to have something like a body language to [distinguish] the Mazda for that time.

'I always look for the movement of the highlights on a car. It's almost like a drama, or a symphony in some cases; like a Jaguar is a symphony. Every moment that lights move on a surface by driving [along], really [tells] the whole story of a car.'

Matano dislikes the use of fussy lines and heavy creases in styling. He said: 'I often think of water, dropping onto the roof, following the curvature, going down the roof to the pillar, to the bottom of the pillar, to whatever. And every time this water has to think which way shall I go down; if the water has to think that way, the design is not right yet. You know, it's not natural yet.

'Because it's a convertible, the

rear end is very important to identify the car. And yet we don't really want to have a spoiler just for the sake of it, so it's there but it's not really obvious.'

During May, the project was considered advanced enough to call a joint meeting between the MANA staff and a large delegation from Japan. As far as the American team was concerned, the project was finished.

A return to Worthing

Once the decision was taken to embrace the lightweight sportscar, Mazda again turned to IAD in England - this time to produce five complete running vehicles (engineering mules), and nine bodyshells for test and evaluation.

The mules didn't have the PPF brace (all will be explained in due course), but otherwise were similar to the future production models. Significant detail changes were made along the way, including the use of a larger fuel tank (the original was far too small to be practical), and redesigning of the hood.

IAD actually carried out the front and rear crash tests which the LWS passed with flying colours. After the Worthing phase in the proceedings was completed, a number of IAD staff were sent to Japan to personally explain problems encountered and make the transition to production as smooth as possible. The Mazda roadster was now a reality.

The synthesis of Man and Horse

The author's theory regarding sportscars has always been that a sportscar has only one purpose - to be driven. Of course, some of the more exotic designs can be looked upon as works of art - and be enjoyed whilst stationary - but, basically speaking, a sportscar is intended to provide driving pleasure.

LWS project Chief Engineer Toshihiko Hirai felt exactly the same way: the Japanese love their cars; they represent personal space in a crowded city and are also something the Japanese can own. Few young people are in a position to buy anything in the housing market other than a tiny flat, as prices are extremely high. Even if somebody does take on a mortgage, repayments often continue well into the third generation of the family!

The car is also an escape into the countryside, or a way of getting to a fishing port; although already very close to the sea (on a foggy day we can hear the boats in Tokyo Bay) my father-in-law will happily travel 70 miles each way, up to three times a week, in order to go fishing on the opposite side of the Chiba peninsula to the one on which we live when in Japan. In other words, even given the prospect of enormous traffic jams at certain times of the day, the automobile is considered a necessity to the enjoyment of life. However, a sportscar is not just a means of transport. It has to look and feel special and make its owner enjoy each and every mile, every corner, every gearchange.

Hirai gathered around him a team of about ten people, including Shinzo Kubo (who had been at MANA for a while, but would nevertheless become Hirai's assistant), Kazuyuki Mitate and Hideaki Tanaka (both of whom had been with the project for some time), Takao Kijima and Masaaki Watanabe. Hirai, described by Bill Livingstone as 'a very professional engineer,' began listing every minute detail that he expected from a sportscar, declaring he would not be happy until all of these criteria had been met. This list took on almost legendary status once the journalists got to hear about it! The concept was originally described as the synthesis of man and vehicle, but this was latter changed to the synthesis of man and horse; Hirai wanted the new Mazda to give the driver the feeling of oneness that exists between a good rider and a thoroughbred stallion.

The final design

The third MANA clay (S-3), arrived in Hiroshima in July 1986, but at that time the studio was packed with other projects. A familiar figure returned to the story when Shunji Tanaka of Design Department No.1 (Hiroshima), took over as Chief Designer.

Initially Tanaka struggled to find a surface plate for the clay; considering the project had still not secured the full support of everyone at Mazda (in a country that is usually so organised), one wonders if this was deliberate. However, one was eventually obtained and in November that year Tanaka started work on the model.

He decided that the car was too heavy-looking for his liking. As he says, he proceeded to 'Take

An interview with Shunji Tanaka (Chief Designer on the M1 Body)

Mr Tanaka: 'Today, there are many open two-seater cars on the market. However, in 1986, there was nothing resembling the open two-seater concept available, and it was hard even to carry out market research effectively. I remember that at the time we really struggled to get this car into production.'

Miho Long: 'Could you tell us your favourite parts of the design, and why?'

Mr Tanaka: 'I like the rear view when the car is open - I believe the rear view of a sportscar has to be cute! I would also suggest the tail lamps, which are as one with the body. I wanted them to resemble a fundo [a balance weight from old-style weighing scales], so I shaved a tail lamp housing myself to get exactly the shape I desired.'

Miho Long: 'Which would you say was the hardest part of the body design to execute?'

Mr Tanaka: 'To create the authentic originality of Mazda and Japan on the body surface. You will notice that the lines enclose an aesthetic consciousness, giving different feelings depending on the angle from which the car is viewed, just like a Noh mask.

'Every time I take up a chisel to create a Noh mask, I always respect the traditional simplicity and perfect curves which have been handed down over the centuries. Many different feelings and wishes are held within the mask, their appearance depending on the light and changing shadows. It is very characteristic of the Japanese, and completely different from the Western notion of expressing perfection concretely.

'I also wanted to enclose the rhythms - peace, motion, and silence - which exist in the Japanese heart, into the form of the sportscar. For peace, I looked towards a statue of the Goddess of Mercy for inspiration, a truly graceful symbol. For motion, I thought of a wild animal when it's hunting, running fast and accurate, and for silence, the tranquillity of nature. I wanted the car to melt into the scenery, reflecting the light over its curved surfaces.

'I wanted to establish a new mould which was dynamic and original, yet distinctly Japanese in its origin - a mixture of sensitivity and modern technology.'

one layer of skin off the MANA model from front to rear.' to reveal a more lithe profile. He insisted that the wheelbase be shortened slightly, causing more than a few problems for the layout engineers (MANA had already lengthened it during development of the third clay), the most obvious of which being the need to move the battery from behind the seats to a new location in the boot. The battery then encroached on luggage space but the stylist stood by his decision. In the end, it helped with weight distribution anyway, so could be regarded as something of a mixed blessing, even though a special lightweight battery was eventually deemed necessary by Hirai.

Tanaka and Hirai had more arguments during development of the final model. Tanaka lowered the cowl height but was prevented by the Chief Engineer from going the extra 20mm he really wanted, although he did manage to change the width of the air intake (when Hirai found out after taking a ruler to the model, it was too late to change it!)

Mazda thought that the car had to have spirit, incorporating the "beauty of Japan," so the brief mentioned a hint of Muromachi culture - a great era in Japanese history that brought about the tea ceremony, *Noh* plays, floral art, the Zen sect, and so on. Tanaka (who was born in 1947 and joined Mazda in 1971) sculpted *Noh* masks as a hobby, and used them for his inspiration. The simple mask itself doesn't change facial expression but as soon as a *Noh* actor wears it, by careful movements the mask

The LWS taking shape in Japan based on MANA's S-3 clay. The Americans had been worried that Tanaka would drop the pop-up headlights; in actual fact, Fukuda (seen pointing in the background) wanted the headlamps placed under clear covers, but regulations dictated that the pop-up arrangement remained in place. Note the 'Minilite' wheels.

Tanaka's finished design. His modifications actually brought the final shape nearer to the original Duo 101 clay submitted by MANA when the project first started. From quite an early stage, Tanaka had removed the black rubbing strip and replaced it with a crease line instead. From this clay, a glassfibre model was built, which was subsequently sent to America to take part in a clinic.

Three views of the glassfibre model that was sent to the States to take part in a clinic held at the Pasadena Convention Centre in 1987.

can be made to show various expressions through the use of light, shadow and different angles.

The modeller, Shigeru Kajiyama, had the unenviable job of interpreting Tanaka's vision to make light dance on the car's profile, regardless of whether it was in motion or stationary. When the clay model was completed, the data was loaded into a computer and it was found that the LWS had 260 different faces (other Mazda cars have around 80 different faces).

After working on the clay model for about three months in between his other work on the Luce, RX-7 and MPV (which were considered by Yamanouchi to be more important at the time), a resin mock-up of the body was produced. This was duly sent to California for appraisal at the end of March 1987, by which time Watanabe and his team had sorted out the vast majority of engineering details. Although staff at MANA were dreading the results (they had been told that Tanaka had been quite brutal with his modifications), they were all suitably impressed and immediately sent a fax through to Hiroshima to convey their congratulations.

It was one thing to impress your colleagues, but the true test came at a clinic held at the Pasadena Convention Centre, when 240 people were invited to give their views on the anonymous vehicle. It received an overwhelming Yes vote which was almost certainly a key factor in the decision to finally go ahead with the project. The importers in America were fully behind the car, so everything was now in place, signed and sealed - there was no turning back.

Engine

A rotary engine was dismissed at the start of the project. Managing Director Takashi Kuroda said that from a marketing point of view (cost was also an important factor) the rotary was better suited to higher-powered, prestige models. Masakatsu Kato was also opposed to the rotary but for different reasons: if an existing unit was to be used the chassis would require costly modifications to enable it to handle the extra power (which would also add a substantial amount of weight), or a new smaller engine would have to be built.

Sensibly, it was decided to adapt an existing unit to cut down on development time and costs.

The fuel-injected 1.6-litre twin-cam engine from the Familia GT was selected and suitably modified to enable the four-cylinder block to be installed longitudinally, instead of in its usual transverse position. Having only recently ushered in the FF layout on the 323 range (which was almost universal on small cars by this time), it is somewhat ironic that this conversion was necessary.

However, the B6-DOHC was found to be less than ideal. Hirai wanted a high- and free-revving engine, and in its standard form this unit, having been tuned to give low-end torque instead of top-end power, was not suitable for its proposed new application. The turbocharged version available in Japan was also quickly discounted.

The water-cooled B6, therefore, was used as a starting point by Kazuo Tominaga and his team. Bore and stroke were retained (78 x

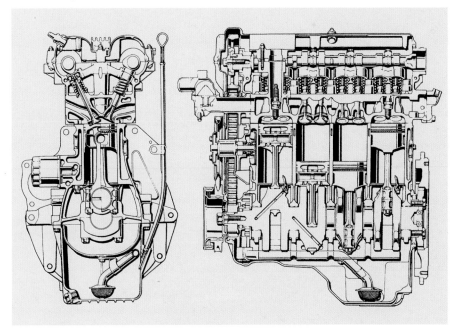

A sectional view of the B6-ZE (RS) engine that was used in the P729 lightweight sportscar.

83.6mm), which gave a cubic capacity of 1597cc. The block, with five main bearings, was of cast-iron, while the head was cast in aluminium alloy. Double-overhead camshafts remained a feature, operating four valves per cylinder, although the timing was changed to allow higher rpm.

The cast-iron crankshaft and flywheel were subtly altered, and this attention to detail resulted in an engine with a 7200rpm red-line. But in typically Japanese fashion, the detailing went much further - even the induction system, cam covers and timing belt cover were stylised to make the engine attractive to look at - and to bear a passable resemblance to Lotus, Alfa Romeo and Fiat twin cam units. Another novel feature was the cast aluminium sump, complete with cooling fins, in best Italian tradition.

Fuel-injection was retained, for although twin-carburettors would have been nice from an aesthetic point of view (as well as following a traditional sportscar line), emission regulations soon scuppered that idea. An L-Jetronic efi system with a pendant-type airflow meter was employed, and Tsunetoshi Yokokura (who had previously worked on the B6-DOHC engine), designed both the intake and exhaust porting and manifolds. To save weight, the free-flow exhaust manifold was produced in steel rather than the more common cast-iron.

Interestingly, instead of using a distributor it was decided to employ a crank angle sensor. Although this computer-linked device cost a fortune compared to

the more traditional ignition set-up, it gave a much smaller and lighter package. Other weight-saving measures included the use of an aluminium and plastic radiator which was cooled by a particularly small electric fan.

The new engine was designated the B6-ZE (RS), and with a compression ratio of 9.4:1 produced 120ps (the Japanese measurement of power which is roughly the same as bhp) at 6500rpm. Maximum torque (of 100lb/ft) came in very high up the rev range at 5500rpm, confirming the sporting nature of the unit. The engine was mounted as far back as possible to bring the weight nearer to the centre of the car.

Drivetrain

The gearbox was developed from the proven M-type five-speed transmission which had seen service in the 2-litre Luce and normally-aspirated RX-7. The main changes concerned the shift linkage which was modified to give a very short stroke between the gears - indeed, when the Mazda engineers had finished, the stubby

gear lever travelled just two inches from any gear into the neutral position, prompting one tester to compare it to operating a rifle bolt. The synchromesh was improved and a subtle 'click' as the lever reached its stop built-in to enhance the positive feel of the 'box.

After reviewing the specifications on a number of sportscars, close and evenly-spaced gear ratios were chosen. With a 4.3:1 final drive, a 3.14:1 first gear gave a maximum of 33mph, while second (1.89:1) allowed 54mph, third (1.33:1) 77mph, the direct fourth gave 102mph and an overdrive top (0.81:1) an estimated 117mph.

The clutch was a single dry plate unit. Power was taken from the gearbox to the back axle via a single-piece propshaft (with the engine located so far back, a two-piece propshaft was deemed unnecessary). A viscous-coupled, limited-slip differential was made available as an option.

Having designed a novel way of bracing the driveline for the forthcoming third generation RX-7 at the end of 1986, Mazda decided

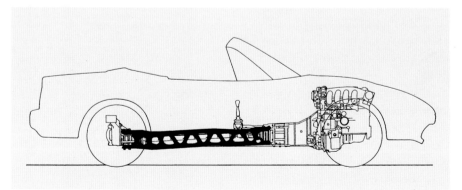

The drivetrain for the LWS was quite short, with the engine mounted a long way back. It was the first car to employ the Power Plant Frame, or PPF. Weighing less than 5kg, it made the engine/gearbox and back axle into an integral unit and made a notable difference to refining power delivery.

to use what it called a Power Plant Frame (or PPF) on the LWS as well. Having tested the idea on an early engineering mule, the system was later adopted for production. The PPF was basically an aluminium bracing piece linking the engine and differential which had been refined and lightened through the use of computer technology; its purpose was to improve throttle response (by stopping the differential unit twisting on its mounts) and reduce drivetrain shudder.

On the subject of throttle response, throttle travel was some 65mm on the LWS, as opposed to the usual 45mm on most Mazdas, and this gave the driver more precise control. The throttle pedal was drilled to evoke memories of earlier sporting machines. (Incidentally, an automatic gearbox would not be offered immediately but was promised for the future.)

Chassis

Having originally been under the auspices of the Technical Research Centre, the job of developing the suspension eventually fell to Takao Kijima and Fumitaka Ando. Kijima was perhaps the ideal person for the job, having thought up the idea of the DTSS system for the second generation RX-7.

It was declared early on that the independent suspension would be via double-wishbones all round; although it would have saved both time and money to use components Mazda already had in service, unequal length A-arms were unrivalled for sportscar suspensions so a new set-up was designed from scratch.

Originally, aluminium alloy suspension components were envisaged, but associated production costs curtailed this line of thought as the LWS was supposed to be an affordable sportscar. Instead, A-arms were fabricated from high-tensile steel sheet, an option which was strong, reasonably light and cheap to manufacture.

Up front, a combined coil spring/gas-filled shock absorber sat in-between the wishbones on each side; an 18mm anti-roll bar was used. At the rear, Kijima - famous for his perfectionism - allowed the forward lower suspension bush to deform slightly under cornering to give the rear wheel a minute amount of toe-in: an ingenious idea. Again, combined coil spring/damper units were used, along with a 12mm diameter anti-roll bar.

Spring rates were completely different to those of the Familia, being 1.6kg/mm at the front and 1.4kg/mm at the rear - the rates for the 323 were quoted as 2.7kg/mm and 2.1kg/mm respectively. Staff from Bilstein spent a great deal of time alongside the Mazda team in Japan on the shock absorber settings, thus ensuring the correct amount of damping for the various types of roads around the world.

The pressed-steel front subframe not only carried the suspension pick-up points, but the steering gear as well. As the engine

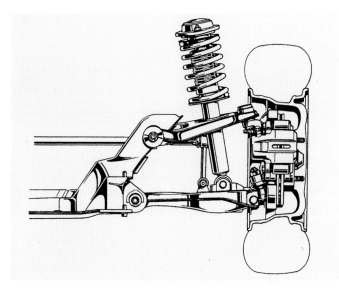

The front suspension.

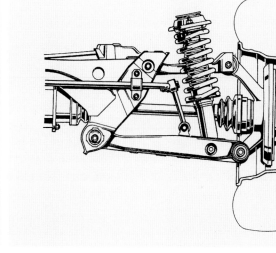

The rear suspension.

29

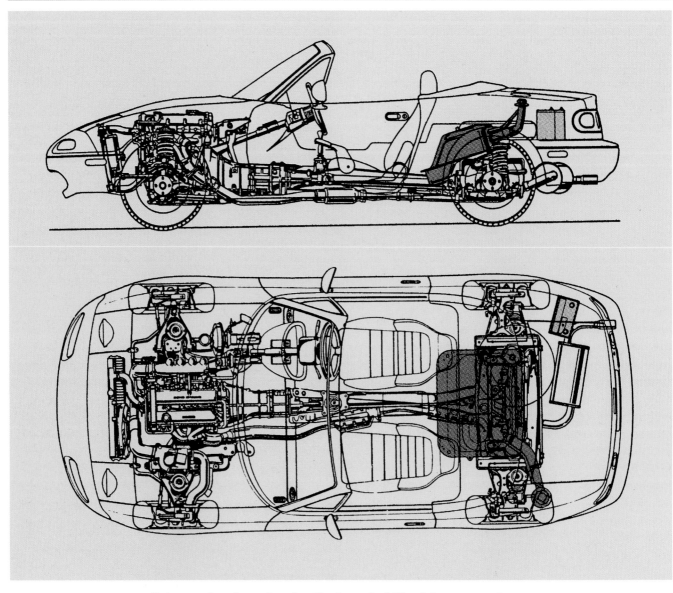

Cutaway drawings showing the layout of Mazda's new sportscar.

was placed so far back, the rack was mounted ahead of it on the front of the subframe. Rack-and-pinion steering was employed, with a ratio of 18.0:1, as opposed to 23.5 on the Familia. This gave 3.3 turns lock-to-lock, but being such a light car, steering effort remained acceptable at slower speeds. The optional power-steering had a 15.3:1 ratio (it was

16.4:1 on the Familia), which translated into just 2.8 turns lock-to-lock.

Drum brakes would probably have been more than adequate for the car's weight and performance (the Porsche 924 had drums at the rear and drums do provide a better handbrake), but for marketing reasons it was decided that discs all round would be better.

The Familia was available with this system and its components provided an ideal basis on which to work. Ventilated discs of 235mm diameter were used at the front and solid items of 231mm at the rear. The pads had a slightly larger area than those of the Familia, and the servo was changed to provide the driver with a more progressive feel.

After the Pasadena clinic, Tanaka set about the subtle detailing to make the car ready for production. The tail was made softer and rear overhang increased by 30mm, and the famous door handles at last made an appearance. This final prototype had raised "Mazda" script on the front bumper, and the shield-shaped badge on the nose carried a star above an abstract bird with opened wings.

Attention to detail was again in evidence; the front calipers were at the trailing edge of the discs, with the rear calipers on the leading edge, thus ensuring that the weight of the braking system was kept within the wheelbase. The handbrake mechanism featured an automatic adjuster and worked on the rear discs.

Finally, the wheels and tyres also came under the spotlight. Shunji Tanaka had come up with an alloy wheel resembling the original Minilite, but given the weight that Hirai wanted, the wheel's would-be manufacturer suggested removing one of the spokes. The 5.5J x 14 alloy wheels were thus destined to have seven spokes instead of eight. Pressed-steel wheels of a similar size were fitted to basic models.

As for the tyres, Mazda approached various companies and asked for a lighter type than those available at the time. Eventually, around 2.5kg was saved on a set of four 185/60 HR14 radials. A spacesaver spare was specified to keep weight to a minimum, and this was placed as close as possible to the rear bulkhead to keep weight distribution correct.

Body

Hirai once again had very strong views about what the body should be like: 'Very light and very stiff.' Masakatsu Kato knew that a fibreglass body and backbone chassis, as used on the IAD prototype, was not an ideal design for mass-production. This idea was not new as Daimler had concluded in 1958 (when looking at the details on the SP250 project) that once production reached 3000 bodies a year, it was cheaper, long-term, to tool-up for steel bodies.

Modern techniques had increased this threshold figure substantially, but the conclusion was basically the same. With high volume sales envisaged for Mazda's LWS, fibreglass was out of the question. Aluminium was also rejected because, although it had an obvious weight advantage, it was a very expensive material compared with steel. However, in Hirai's quest for weight reduction, some aluminium would eventually be used for panelwork.

Mazda's GNC-2 computer programme was used to enable the engineers to reduce weight whilst at the same time retain vehicle rigidity. The car's body was an incredibly light structure, but strength was guaranteed by the thoroughness of Hirai's team. On average, stress measurements are taken and analyzed at approximately 5000 points, but in the case of the LWS project no less than 8900 readings were used to ensure the body would be free of the problems - such as scuttle shake - one usually associates with open cars. Designing the car as a convertible from day one was an added advantage of course, as converting a coupé into a drophead always involves compromises.

The bodyshell was of all-steel welded unitary construction, although to reduce weight forward of the centreline it featured an aluminium bonnet. The bootlid was actually made out of thinner gauge steel than was the rest of the body. The steel part of the car accounted for just 16 per cent of the P729's total weight. With so many subtle lines, Naoyuki Ikemizu said the tooling for the panels was very difficult to make.

The front bumpers were faced with urethane, while the rear bumper used polypropylene. Both were backed by impact-absorbing, blow-moulded plastic, and mounted on the bodyshell via lightweight polycarbonate brackets. This arrangement, compared with more traditional bumpers, significantly reduced weight at the car's extremities. In addition, side impact bars within the doors were tubular to further reduce weight.

Overall dimensions of the roadster were: length 3970mm; width 1675mm; height 1235mm and wheelbase 2265mm. Ground clearance was 140mm, while the front and rear track were 1405 and 1420mm respectively. Although not particularly impressive by today's standards, for an open car the Cd figure of 0.38 was more than respectable, although it did rise to 0.44 with the hood down. Luggage space, incidentally, amounted to just six cubic feet.

Interior

Above all, the cockpit was designed to be functional, and rightfully so - it was said to represent the simplicity of a Japanese tea room. Of course, weight was kept to a bare minimum; also the interior was fully trimmed. Early designs had been a little too futuristic, so Kenji Matsuo decided to resort to a Ţ-shaped theme like that found on sportscars from the past.

The cluster of instruments contained five main gauges, with a large 8000rpm tachometer on the left and matching speedo to the right. The small oil pressure gauge sat between and above them, while the similar-sized fuel and temperature gauges were low down on each side. The two larger dials had chrome surrounds to make them stand out.

Mazda advertising from the mid-1980s. Mazda team members were certainly perfectionists regarding the LWS project.

In the tail of the T-shaped arrangement were two of the four eyeballs for ventilation (the others were at each extremity of the fascia) and heater controls, both of which were sourced from the first generation RX-7. However, as *Car Styling* said: 'The sense of unity has been pursued by fully using the motif of a circle as seen in the meters and ventilator grille, but the basic touch of quality is somewhat unsatisfactory.'

High-backed seats were selected with integral headrests - many magazines (and even a few people within the company) commented on the somewhat tight "cosy" feel within the cockpit, but most testers were happy with the support provided by the seating.

The steering wheel was a

four-spoke affair for America (to allow for an airbag), or a three-spoke design elsewhere. A leather-wrapped wheel was available one way or another - either as standard or as an option - in most markets.

At Hirai's insistence, the sunvisors were made to fold in two to stop them showing over the top rail (although eventually more traditional items were adopted, presumably to save on production costs). At the other extreme, door trims were very basic and the cheap-looking handles inside were a stark contrast to the Tanaka-styled items found outside. Indeed, Tanaka commented that a lot of effort had gone into the exterior, but the interior had been produced with cost as a prime consideration.

Finishing touches

By September 1987 drawings had been submitted to enable trial manufacture, and the resulting prototype was eventually passed on to Hirotaka Tachibana of the Experimental Department. Tachibana, who had been with Mazda for many years after leaving the Bridgestone concern, wanted the car to feel responsive, and had the suspension tuned so that it performed its best at around 60mph - a speed that the vast majority of people can enjoy but still keep within the law. He wanted a forgiving vehicle that would reward drivers whatever their level of skill, and testing was carried out at the Miyoshi proving ground as well as on the roads of America and Europe.

In the Psychoacoustics Lab in Japan, a large number of people were asked their opinions on various exhaust notes. Those involved in the tests all came from different age groups and back-grounds, representing a fair cross-section of potential buyers. They recorded their thoughts on set format pre-printed sheets which gave the engineers a good idea of what the public expected the ideal sportscar to sound like. Makoto Shinhama designed and built an exhaust system out of stainless steel to suit. In line with Hirai's drive to keep everything as light as possible - including the standard three-way catalytic converter - the system weighed less than 18kg.

As well as having the right exhaust note, Hirai stated that a tight seating arrangement was necessary to give the car the intimate atmosphere he wanted. He said: 'In the course of the development, we are apt to enlarge a vehicle by expecting too much. But then, the sense of unity between the rider and the vehicle is lost. That is why we adhered to limits for all aspects of this car.' Even so, he was quick to point out that due to the Mazda's wider track, there was more room in the cockpit than in the average British sportscar of the 1960s.

The roadster was designed to give the full feeling of an open car. That statement may seem a little obvious, but one has only to think of vehicles like the RX-7 Cabriolet and the Jaguar XJ-S Convertible, where the occupants are cosseted from draughts and direct airflow, and compare them to the wind-in-the-hair experience one gets with a sportscar from the '60s, for instance.

Mazda went to extraordinary lengths to get the movement of air

A smiling Tachibana talking over the finer points of the LWS with Hirai (seated). The relationship between the two was not always this cordial - a fact that came to the attention of the MD, Michinori Yamanouchi. He delivered them an ultimatum: work together or leave the project that meant so much to both of them.

in the cockpit right. The large door mirrors were shaped and positioned so that occupants didn't get draughts on their shoulders; it has even been said that a long-haired lady was taken to Miyoshi to see how medium-speed runs affected her hairstyle!

Despite having completed its 20 millionth vehicle, as far as the hood was concerned Mazda hadn't had a great deal of experience in this field. The Familia Cabriolet had not been particularly popular, and introduction of the RX-7 Cabriolet, launched to commemorate the 20th anniversary of Mazda's rotary-engined automobiles, didn't occur until 1987 (1988 Model Year in the States).

It was declared at a very early stage that the hood had to be designed in such a way that it could be operated quickly with just one hand, rather like that found on the Alfa Romeo Spiders. A lightweight frame was duly designed, covered with an unlined material which incorporated a vinyl chloride rear window. The latter could be unfastened via a zip to allow for extra ventilation, or for when the hood was lowered. With the soft-top up (or with a hardtop in place), it was found that noise was amplified within the cockpit, but the same is true of virtually all convertibles.

In addition to the standard soft-top (which was found to be both taut and weatherproof in practice), an optional hardtop was made available. An SMC plastic was employed for its construction to give the best combination of light weight and strength, but first attempts were far from satisfactory. Quality and colour matching were improved, but even then Mazda was not entirely happy with all the shades proposed, so only red was sold initially. With a glass rear screen, it fixed at six points and made the body noticeably more rigid.

After all had been finalised, the basic car weighed just 940kg; even then, Hirai thought it possible to shed more weight. However, Hirai must have been pleased with weight distribution - most of it being low down and within the wheelbase, just as he wished - with 52 per cent over the front wheels and 48 per cent over the rear. It was almost a perfectly balanced car.

The MX-04

At the 1987 Tokyo Show, Mazda displayed the MX-04. The MX-02 and 03 had been practical cars with seating for four, featuring advanced but nonetheless conservative styling. The MX-04 was completely different. Powered by a 150bhp rotary engine, the MX-04 could be fitted with any of three fibreglass body styles: a closed coupé or a choice of two roadsters.

Although the MX-04 was not the prettiest car ever produced by Mazda, some of its features gave a number of clues to the future that few picked up on - independent suspension by unequal-length upper and lower arms, and a backbone chassis developed by Masakatsu Kato. It is interesting that the headlights on the MX-04 were fixed rather than pop-up, giving the car a similar frontal aspect to the second generation MX-5.

Another debutant at the 1987 Tokyo Show (the last to be held at the Harumi site) was the mid-engined Suzuki R/S3. This was the second time in a row that Suzuki had displayed an LWS as its concept car design, and on both occasions they looked suitable for production, giving Fukuda more than a little cause for concern. Maybe Mazda would have a competitor in the near future?

In fact, Mazda knew it was guaranteed at least one competitor, as Ford (who owned 24.5 per cent of Mazda at the time) was planning to bring out the Mercury Capri - a fwd convertible using a large number of components sourced from the Familia. Based on Ford's Barchetta, an exhibit at the

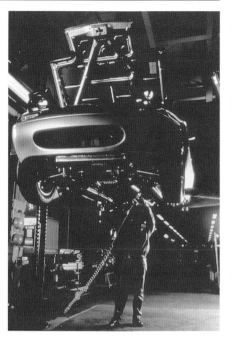

The pilot build at Hiroshima. A small number of journalists from influential magazines were allowed to drive this series of 12 vehicles well in advance of the launch.

1983 Frankfurt Show, it was built in Ford's plant in Australia. Although announced early in 1988, it wasn't introduced until the end of 1989.

The pilot build

The Mazda team must have held its breath when Bitter announced a two-seater convertible at the 1988 Geneva Show. It looked very similar to the P729 and was said to be ready for production, with sales to the US in preparation. Fortunately for Mazda, it was a typical Bitter product - upmarket (and therefore expensive), powered by a large Opel engine and very low-volume.

Shortly after this, the pilot build process began, with 12 cars being put together by hand at the plant in Hiroshima. These were

The new Mazda sportscar with (from left to right), Tom Matano, Wu-Huang Chin, Mark Jordan and Shunji Tanaka. It was to be known as the Eunos Roadster in Japan, the MX-5 Miata in the States and the MX-5 in all other markets.

labelled S1-1 through to S1-12 and would be the vehicles tested by a select number of journalists well in advance of the launch.

Dennis Simanaitis of *Road & Track* was one of those lucky enough to be chosen to test the three vehicles Mazda had provided for the day. 'Last summer I was invited to Mazda's Miyoshi proving grounds to drive a prototype of the company's all-new lightweight sportscar ...

'It helped assess how brilliantly conceived and executed this new car is. Its convertible top is a good example. It had to be easily erected or stowed from the driver seat. It required a latching mechanism that was easy to use. Erected, it had to offer perfect

sealing up to 80mph. Down, it had to stow completely below the car's rear deck line. These engineering criteria give a perfect description of the Miata's soft-top, developed in conjunction with the British design specialist IAD. Its latches, for instance, are large and of a novel over-centre sort that don't need Godzilla for actuation. Though not a heavily padded top of the Germanic idiom, Mazda does get its top materials from the same firm supplying Volkswagen and BMW ...

'Twist the key and you're rewarded with a pleasant burble from the Miata's 1597cc fuel-injected inline-four, essentially the same dohc four-valver powering sporty 323s. One change, a

lightened flywheel, emphasizes its sportscar intent ... Snick the shift lever into first, and you'll experience another element on Mr Hirai's list. The shifter and its actuation are super short and wonderfully positive ...

'Consulting Mr Hirai's list again, engineers worked for a feeling of directness between throttle and rear wheels. I believe a lot of this driveline integrity is achieved by an artfully cast piece of aluminum that connects the engine, transmission and final drive. Check off another goal successfully met. Handling goals occupy a good portion of the list, and it's in this area that the Miata impresses me the most. Its combination of communication, responsiveness, predictability and forgiveness makes it the best-handling two-seater I've driven in recent memory - and my memory for such things is good ... It was an absolute delight and my post-drive debriefing with Mazda engineers probably sounded like over-hyped ad copy ...'

In Japan, the June 1989 edition of *Car Magazine* noted that 'Although from the outside it looks like a British lightweight sports of the 1960s, to drive it is definitely a car from today. After driving it,

one is left with a feeling of happiness.'

In the meantime, importation and distribution of Mazdas in the States was consolidated with the establishment of Mazda Motor of America Inc. (MMA), and the completion of the Mazda R&D of North America Inc. facility in Irvine, California (MRA, *née* MANA). Unfortunately, despite Mazda's best efforts to keep the new car under wraps until its official launch, the cover of *Auto Week* carried a picture of the P729,

as well as an article inside; this was at the end of November - a long way ahead of Mazda's planned publicity campaign.

What's in a name?

Throughout the development of Mazda's new sportscar, it had been given a number of codenames and designations. Firstly, it was known simply as the LWS, but as time passed and the LWS was declared an official 'OGG' project, it was given the code P729. Interestingly, despite the second generation RX-7

MX-5 production at the Hiroshima Plant Complex, where it was built alongside the RX-7 and a number of other cars in the Mazda range.

having already been granted production status, and the fact that work on it was started well in advance of P729 (so one would expect a lower number), it was given the code P747.

Whatever, as P729 took shape, a number of prototypes were built. The first full-size clay produced by MANA was christened the Duo 101 by the Americans, but should probably be called the S-1 to comply with future policy.

The handbuilt machine constructed by IAD was designated V705; the V denoting that it was a one-off prototype. Shortly after, the second full-sized styling clay produced at MANA was designated S-2, and the final one, naturally, was S-3, after which, the project was sent to Hiroshima.

The engineering mules, also constructed by IAD in England, were known by the code M-1, the M denoting mechanical. Still using the P729 code, the project was taken through its final stages in Hiroshima until 12 handbuilt prototypes were constructed in 1988. These were named S1-1, S1-2, and so on up to S1-12, but should not be confused with the MANA styling clays.

One would think that once the new sportscar reached production status, things would become simpler. However, three different names were chosen for different markets.

The MX series of concept cars (the MX-02 Show Car in 1983, followed by the MX-03 in 1985 and MX-04 in 1987) had the right image, and the LWS was so unlike the rest of the Mazda range that a new designation was needed anyway. The new sportscar was therefore christened the MX-5 (presumably MX-05 was dropped as it fails to roll off the tongue quite so easily).

So, the MX-5 was the name used in all markets - I'm afraid not! Both America and Japan decided they needed something different.

In the USA, Laguna was a hot favourite, but then marketing boss Rod Bymaster came across the word "meed" in the dictionary. Today, this means "reward" or "due amount of praise," but Mazda Meed just doesn't appeal. However, apparently its origins lie in an old German word - Miata. It was perfect; the new Mazda would be christened the Miata. However, there was a slight problem - in Japan there was a company with a very similar-sounding name.

The Miyata business was founded in Tokyo in 1880, concerning itself mainly with the production of armaments. Although better-known nowadays as a manufacturer of bicycles (the company has been in the trade for over a century, after all), Eisuke Miyata had also built a small two-cylinder car as early as 1909. Just before the Second World War, a number of Asahi light cars were constructed, and the company was heavily involved with motorbikes, too. Having produced its first Triumph-based machine in 1913 (also known as the Asahi), it finally stopped building motorcycles in the mid-1960s.

After some negotiations it was agreed that the official designation would be 'MX-5 Miata' in the States, but the home market would use a different name. On 4 April 1989, Mazda set up the Eunos and Autozam sales channels to augment those already in place. This splitting of the line-up is common practice in Japan where home market ranges are so extensive (Toyota currently lists 45 basic models, for instance, before moving into commercials). Basically, it gives the dealers the opportunity to compete in different market sectors.

Anyway, after much deliberation, it was decided to call the new sportscar the Eunos Roadster and to sell it through Eunos dealerships. The word Eunos, apparently, comes from a combination of the latin word for joy and an abbreviation of numbers. Expressed another way, it could be taken to mean a collection of joy! At last, the LWS had its proper names.

Looking back, Toshihiko Hirai said: 'There were times when a small breeze from the wrong direction could have blown the project away,' but the future of the car that meant so much to him was now secure and three months ahead of schedule.

MX-5 production was to take place at the Hiroshima Plant Complex (opened in November 1966), where it was built alongside the RX-7 and a number of other cars in the Mazda range.

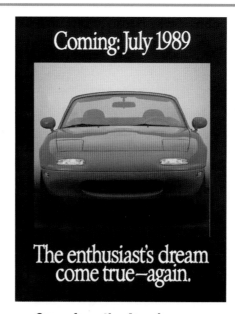

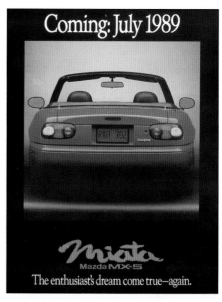

Cover from the American pre-launch brochure, describing the car as 'The enthusiast's dream come true - again.'

The rear of the pre-launch brochure aptly showing the tail of the Miata. (There were actually two different rear panels to suit the shapes and sizes of numberplates for any given market.)

After years of preparation, the Mazda MX-5 was finally unveiled at the 1989 Chicago Auto Show in the United States. The event, which opened on 10 February, saw the debut of two other important Japanese cars - the Nissan 300ZX and Honda's NSX supercar - so some of the initial impact could so easily have been lost. However, at less than $14,000, the Miata was in a completely different price-bracket, so a clash was avoided.

To help the Miata get even more press coverage, the so-called 'Club Racer' was shown alongside the production models. There was a link here with the launch of the original RX-7, when Toyo Kogyo had put a "competition version" of the new car on display. This was something that nobody seemed to pick up on, presumably because they were too busy filling column

inches on the latest Mazda to look into the past. Finished in a bright yellow hue, it seemed that every magazine in the country featured at least one picture of the Club Racer.

The production models were the most important to Mazda, of course, as it was these that would give a return on its investment. The marketing was extremely clever - well co-ordinated and, above all, very thorough. The American public was bombarded with Miata stories almost every-where it looked in a newsagents and people couldn't even sit down for a quiet evening in front of the television without seeing one.

American television advertising showed ghosted images of an Austin-Healey and Triumph TR in the dark. Then day broke with a new, bright red MX-5 sitting in the sunshine outside the garage. The idea behind this was that the British cars had to have maintenance or be repaired well into the night, whereas the Mazda owner just got into his car and drove it away. As Bob Hall once said, although the British sportscars of the 1960s had a certain charm, reliability was not a strong point ...

Although the Mazda didn't officially go on sale until July, by mid-1989 *Road & Track* was already voting the Miata as one of the world's best cars, lined up alongside the Ferrari Testarossa, Mercedes-Benz 300E, Chevrolet Corvette ZR1 and Porsche 911 Carrera 4. In one paragraph, the MX-5 project was summed up perfectly: 'Just born and already a star. What does that say about the MX-5? That it stole the hearts (and votes) of nine smitten staffers. That in typical Japanese fashion, Mazda has done its homework and come up with a design and a concept that time has all but forgotten: the basic, front-engine, rear-drive, open-top affordable sportscar.'

Shortly after launch the same magazine had said: 'Mazda hopes to attract 40,000 buyers per year, which sounds a bit optimistic.' But the timing was perfect; the Hiroshima concern had beaten the competition into a market many thought had disappeared.

Miata fever seemed to grip the States. As *Road & Track* said: 'More than any other car in recent memory - and even fairly distant memory - the Mazda Miata has created a stir of almost embarrassing proportions ...' Deposits were being taken months in advance, and rumours soon spread of

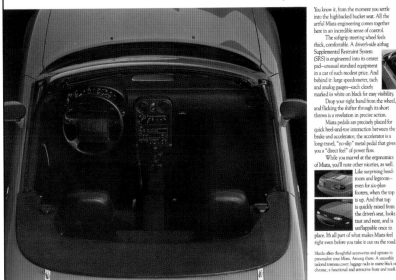

A page from the first American catalogue showing the snug cockpit of the Miata.

people paying ridiculous premiums - it was a re-run of 1970, when the Datsun 240Z first hit the American scene. Demand outstripping supply was the root cause once again, as only 20,000 units were scheduled for the US in the first year.

The American market was given the 1.6-litre twin-cam engine (much the same as that found in other parts of the world), with a five-speed manual gearbox. Introduced at $13,800 (although few people managed to get one for that price), one of the few standard features that made a concession to modernity was a driver's side airbag, but that was the way things were intended to be with the MX-5 - a full set of instruments and comfortable adjustable seats were far more important. One journalist remarked that the MX-5 was 'a refreshing throwback to simpler times.'

The basic list price was indeed cheap. Mazda promoted its new convertible with the phrase 'The return of the affordable sportscar.' The RX-7 now ranged from $17,880 to a mighty $26,530. On the other hand, if one looks at the other two Japanese sportscars launched in Chicago, the Z-cars had become progressively more and more expensive (the Z32 type 300ZX was launched at $27,300 in its cheapest form), and the NSX made the Z look a snip, even at that price.

A number of options were available for the MX-5. For starters, there were two different packages: Package A, priced at $1145, included alloy wheels, a Panasonic stereo radio/cassette,

Another double-page spread from the first catalogue issued in the States (printed in July 1989). The heading proclaims: "Just born and already a star ..."

The 1990 Model Year Miata with optional hardtop in place. In the USA, the hardtop was only available in red, but in the author's opinion it was a very attractive package.

leather-rimmed steering wheel and power-assisted steering, while Package B (at $1730) included everything in Package A plus cruise control, headrest speakers and electric windows.

Air conditioning, a viscous limited-slip differential, a CD player and fitted overmats were offered separately. The air conditioning was $795, while LSD was a very reasonable $250. The CD, at a hefty $600, reflected the fact that this type of stereo equipment was then quite novel in a car. Floor mats were just $59.

A 1990 Model Year Miata, which was the name given to the MX-5 for the American market. Note the optional seven-spoke alloys.

A number of dealer-installed accessories were available, including a tonneau cover, a protective front-end mask (known affectionately in the States as a 'bra'), front and rear spoilers, side skirts, a luggage rack for the bootlid and various alarm systems.

A removable hardtop was also listed which cost $1100 extra but was sold in red only after Mazda had trouble matching the blue and white pigments initially (the other two shades eventually followed in the spring of 1990). On the subject of colour schemes, three colours were available in the States - Classic Red, Crystal White and Mariner Blue. Yellow and British Racing Green were ex-pected to join the line-up in the future, but it was a silver hue (Silver Stone Metallic) that made it to the market first.

Press reaction in the States

The July 1989 edition of *Road & Track* carried an article that was to set the scene across the whole of America. One journalist after another seemed to fall under the MX-5's spell: 'The Miata's fuel-injected 116bhp dohc four (the only engine Mazda offers) keeps giving all the way up to its 7000rpm redline. Musically, the engine is a perfect tenor, serenading the driver lustily to 6200rpm, where the exhaust note begins to sour. This engine is mated exclusively (no automatic transmission offered) to a terrific five-speed manual with super-short throws and a precise feel.'

The magazine managed a 0-60 time of 9.5 seconds (around a second slower than the Toyota MR2 or Honda's CRX Si), whilst top speed was recorded at 117mph and the standing quarter covered in 17.0 (with an 81.5mph terminal speed).

These figures were nothing if not respectable, but Mazda looked at all round performance, not just 0-60 times. This policy is something that Porsche has always adhered to - making a complete package rather than a vehicle that is quick only in a straight line - a car has to feel right, too.

In this respect, the Mazda team had succeeded. Like every magazine in America, the team was more than happy with the overall package. Compared to the competition, it said 'The Miata's four-wheel disc brakes don't seem to give it any relative stopping advantage, either. The brake feel is very good, however, with excellent communication between the pedal, brakes and tyres ...

'We even had the convertible top up one time to check on the headroom (we found plenty) ... The top's sealing against rain and wind noise was superb. With the top down, the swirling winds wafted freely through the driving compartment, but did so without buffeting the occupants to distraction or noisily ruining conversation. It is also important to point out that chassis flexing, a crucial consideration (and problem spot) on convertibles, was virtually non-existent in the Miata ...'

Hailing 'the return of the honest sports car," *Car & Driver* was equally enthusiastic. 'If the new Mazda MX-5 Miata was any more talented and tempting, buying one would be illegal ... The Miata delivers an overload of the kind of pure, unadulterated sports car pleasure that became all but extinct 20 years ago.'

Although probably just a touch biased as a member of the MANA organisation, Bob Hall summed up most of these feelings when he described his first drive home from the office: 'The very first time I drove a Miata home was kind of an interesting experi-ence. Normally my ride home is about 28 miles, and it takes me 35 to 40 minutes. I stretched it out just a little bit that evening - I think it went to about 137 or 138 miles!' As for the bodywork, Mark Stehrenberger carried out an expert and in-depth styling analysis. Finding very few faults, he eventually declared: 'It's a winner!'

Of the 263,000 Mazdas sold in the USA during 1989 (Mazda's record sales period in the States at that time), no less than 23,052 of them were Miatas, despite it arriving midway through the year. 1990 was a poor year for Mazda Stateside, but nonetheless Miata sales still continued to rise - helped, no doubt - by the addition to the line-up of silver paintwork and automatic transmission in March. Press reaction had been extremely favourable: the MX-5 Miata was a far greater success than anyone had anticipated.

The home market

Car design was becoming more fashion-driven, especially in Japan, a country very responsive to trends. Booms seem to come and go overnight, but when they do happen they're extremely intense. The retro-boom seems to have lingered longer than most, however.

Starting in the early to mid-1980s, one of the first car manufac-turers to cash in on this particular boom was Nissan, with the March (or Micra) providing the basis for the highly-successful Be-1 launched in 1985. After this there was the Figaro and then the Pau. The Figaro proved so popular that in the end Nissan had to hold a lottery to decide who could have one!

A number of firms followed Nissan's lead, and even at the 1997 Tokyo Show there were still an enormous number of exhibits featuring the retro-look. However, with the retro-boom in full swing in Japan when Mazda launched the MX-5, it meant that timing was not only good in America but also in Japan.

Having been officially announced on 3 July (deposits were taken from the 5th of that month), the MX-5 eventually went on sale in Japan on 1 September. Oddly, the full four-day press launch wasn't held until 4 July, despite a number of magazines already covering the car before-hand. The launch took place in Hakone and the Mazda design team was present, along with 15 cars. As mentioned earlier, the MX-5 was named the Eunos Roadster in its native country, and was sold exclusively through the Eunos sales channel.

The home market had a standard 1.6-litre model (which started at chassis NA6CE-100021), and the so-called 1.6-litre Special Package version, the first of which carried chassis number NA6CE-100022. The basic model (priced at 1,748,000 yen) weighed in at just 940kg and was indeed basic. The Special Package added 10kg in weight and a further 150,000 yen. The Special Package included powered-steering, seven-spoke 5.5J x 14 alloy wheels, electric windows and a Momo leather-rimmed steering wheel.

Major options included air

兆し。

クルマはもっと豊かになれる。
その主張を、
ユーノスはまず "ロードスター" で表現します。

EUNOS / CITROËN

EUNOS ROADSTER
〈スペシャルパッケージ装着車〉

まったく 新しい カーチャネル "ユーノス" 9月オープン。

クルマそのもののよさを純粋に愉しみ、深く吟味する時代へ。今クルマが、クルマをとりまく環境が、大きく変わろうとしています。そんな時代の動きに先駆けて "ユーノス" は誕生しました。ただ奇をてらうのではなく、大人のときめきに応えられるような個性豊かなクルマを。私たちユーノスは「本物」だけをお届けしたいと考えます。そこで、まず噂のライトスポーツ "ユーノスロードスター" の予約受付を開始。また9月からはフランスの名車 "シトロエンBX" の販売も予定しております。クルマ社会がさらに面白くなりそうな「兆し」、ユーノスにご期待ください。

CITROËN BX

EunoS

株式会社 ユーノス

conditioning (150,000 yen), a detachable hardtop (165,000 yen), a CD player (62,000 yen) and limited-slip differential. Other components mentioned at the launch included a wood-rimmed Nardi steering wheel with matching gearknob and handbrake handle (which didn't appear for some time), a polished cam cover, chrome door mirrors and an uprated suspension kit. The 5.5J alloys mentioned earlier were augmented by two 6J x 14 wheels - a Mazdaspeed five-spoke design

DIMENSIONS ●Overall length:3970mm ●Overall width:1675mm ●Overall height:1235mm ●Wheelbase:2265mm ●Tread(Front/Rear):1405mm/1420mm ●Ground clearance:140mm

Interior of the Special Package model, shown here with optional air conditioning and CD player. Unlike in America, in Japan the detachable hardtop was available in either red or black.

and a 17-spoke from the SPA concern.

Minor items included polished treadplates with the "Roadster" logo, a front air dam skirt (provided by the factory in black), projector lamps (situated in the air intake), rear mudflaps, an alloy gearshift gaiter retainer, an alloy handbrake lever handle and door-edge mouldings. As well as Eunos clothing and luggage, perhaps the trendiest accessory was a TAG Heuer 2000 Series watch with "Eunos" stamped into the strap's security clip.

Reviewing the new Mazda in June 1989, Shigeharu Kumakura of *Car Graphic* thought it was a bit 'tail happy' and that the engine could do with a little more refinement, but he immediately fell in love with the interior. The tester also commented on the lack of scuttle shake, the excellent soft-top (claiming there was no real need for a hardtop), and was pleased with the movement of air within the cockpit whilst the hood was down. Interestingly, the feel of the gearshift was highly commended, although gear spacing between second and third and third to fourth was felt to be not close enough.

In its September 1989 edition, *Motor Fan* pointed out that there were two types of sportscar - one that lets you enjoy the sensation of speed, the other the feel of control.

The MX-5 fell into the category of driver enjoyment through control.

It was noted that the Eunos Roadster was not a fast car, but the overall mood was good. Little things were very pleasing: 'the exhaust note under 4000rpm is very quiet, but over this it becomes musical. The delivery of torque is very smooth, and the whole car reacts to each movement of the accelerator.' The tester was also

POWER TRAIN ●1597cc DOHC 16-valve engine ●Compression ratio:9.4
●Max. power:120ps/6500rpm(NET) ●Max. torque:14.0kg-m/5500rpm ●EGI
●5-speed manual transmission ●Power Plant Frame

The home market Special Package model as seen at the time of the Eunos Roadster's official debut. As Car Styling pointed out, the number-plate is a little conspicuous and the pop-up headlights are perhaps a tad old-fashioned. (Although aerodynamics are improved when the covers are closed, airflow is disturbed when the lights are in use; in addition, the operating mechanism is quite heavy.)

happy with the classical sportscar interior, but thought the seats needed to give the driver more support during hard cornering.

Japanese car firms always seem to intend a sportscar boot to have enough room for two golf bags. The new Mazda was no exception although after the battery was moved from its original location behind the seats providing this amount of space was no longer possible. A lack of luggage capacity was one of the few major problems identified by journalists and end users, but Mazda knew the problem existed and would solve it eventually.

It looked as if Mazda had timed the promotional build-up to perfection. Like America, virtually all forms of media seemed to feature the MX-5, and this completely overshadowed the launch of a serious competitor - the Suzuki Cappuccino, a lightweight two-seater powered by a 658cc turbocharged engine. First displayed at the 1989 Tokyo Show, it failed to grab the headlines after the Mazda stole all the glory. For this reason, it wasn't until November 1991 that it finally went on sale. At just 1,458,000 yen, it was very reasonably priced.

Automatic transmission was added to the Eunos Roadster options listing in March 1990. Priced at just 40,000 yen extra, it added 30kg to the overall weight of the vehicle and was associated with a slightly detuned engine (to bring in maximum torque at 4500rpm). It was obvious that this combination would hardly place it in the supercar league, but in a country where most cars are fitted with two pedals instead of three, it made a lot of sense to offer the option. A Special Package model was the first to receive the four-speed automatic gearbox (chassis NA6CE-113858), although it was also available on the standard version, the first car being NA6CE-114565.

Available in Classic Red, Crystal White, Silver Stone Metallic, or Mariner Blue, the

高回転型1600DOHC16バルブ＋パワープラントフレーム
ダイレクトレスポンスの快感。

パワーユニットは、最高出力120ps/6500rpm（※ネット）、最大トルク14.0kg-m/5500rpmを発生する1600ccDOHC16バルブ。可変吸気機構すら持たない純粋な自然吸気エンジンだ。そして、高回転域へスムーズに連続するトルクカーブを得るため、高回転設定のカムタイミング、テーパー化した吸気ポートなどを採用。レッドゾーン7200rpmまで一気に吹け上がる回転特性を実現している。駆動方式は、無論FR。しかも、トランスミッションとデフをリジッドに結合するアルミ製P.P.F.（パワープラントフレーム）を採用。これによるエンジン/トランスミッション/デフの一体化が、スロットルレスポンスをよりダイレクトなものにするために貢献している。
※「ネット」とはエンジンを車両搭載状態で測定したものです。

4輪ダブルウィッシュボーン＋オープン専用・高剛性軽量ボディ。
ダイレクトハンドリングの快感。

サスペンションは、4輪ダブルウィッシュボーン。路面に対するタイヤのジオメトリーをつねに適正に保ち、すぐれたロードホールディングを発揮する。また、ヨー慣性モーメントの低減を図るため、重量をできるかぎり車体中央の重心点方向に寄せてレイアウト。操舵にリニアに対応するダイレクトなハンドリングフィールをさらに高めている。そして、最新のコンピューター解析技術を駆使したオープン専用設計ボディ。軽量化とともに、オープンボディの常識をはるかに凌ぐ高剛性を実現した。さらに、アルミ製ボンネットフードやステンレス製エグゾーストパイプ、樹脂製バンパー、小型シールドバッテリーの採用など、軽量化を追求している。

Above & opposite: Another double-page spread showing the technical specifications for the home market, as well as the 1.6-litre four-cylinder engine and LWS 'chassis.' Note the PPF running down the centre and the seven-spoke wheel design, chosen because seven spokes weigh less than the Minilite's traditional eight.

Eunos Roadster was an immediate hit. Between September 1989 and the end of that year, no less than 9307 were sold. In 1990, this figure nearly tripled, over 25,000 Roadsters finding new homes in the Land of the Rising Sun.

Other markets 1989
Apart from America and Japan, the only other markets to get the MX-5 in 1989 were Canada and Australia. For many years, Canadian vehicles have usually complied quite closely to American specifi-

cation models and the MX-5 was no exception. Almost 3000 found their way to Canadian buyers in the first year of production, a figure that rose to nearer 4000 in 1990.

As for Australia, its model was very similiar to Japanese specification cars in that both had right-hand drive. By this time, emission regulations were becoming much the same across the world (all countries were stricter than they had been in the 1970s and international regulations not

now very different to those required in California), so this no longer meant special exhaust equipment for certain markets. Australia is quite close to Japan (at least compared with America or Europe), so shipping is much quicker.

Sales started in Australia in October 1989 (just one model was listed), and by the end of the year 621 had been sold. Naturally, with a full year's sales in 1990, this figure increased - in fact, by no less than 233 per cent. Shortly after the

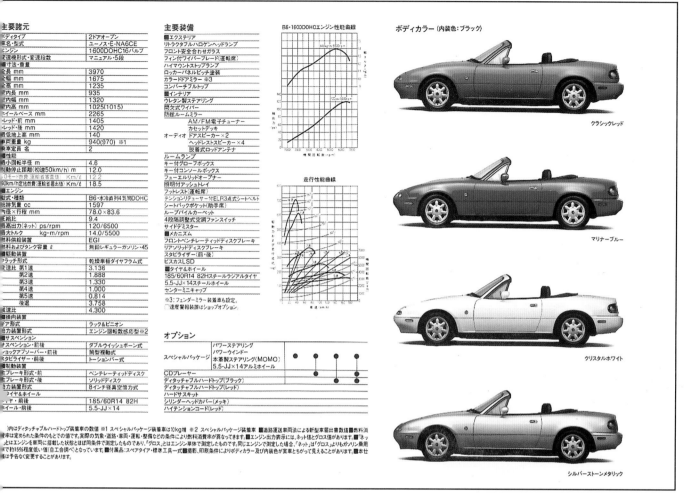

主要諸元

項目	諸元
ボディタイプ	2ドアオープン
車名・型式	ユーノス・E-NA6CE
エンジン	1600DOHC16バルブ
変速機形式・変速段数	マニュアル・5段
寸法・重量	
全長 mm	3970
全幅 mm	1675
全高 mm	1235
室内長 mm	935
室内幅 mm	1320
室内高 mm	1025(1015)
ホイールベース mm	2265
トレッド・前 mm	1405
トレッド・後 mm	1420
最低地上高 mm	140
車両重量 kg	940(970) ※1
乗車定員 名	2
性能	
最小回転半径 m	4.6
制動停止距離(初速50km/h) m	12.0
10モード燃費(運輸省審査値) Km/ℓ	12.2
定地燃費(60km/h定地走行燃費 運輸省届出値) Km/ℓ	18.5
エンジン	
型式・種類	B6・水冷直列4気筒DOHC
総排気量 cc	1597
内径×行程 mm	78.0×83.6
圧縮比	9.4
最高出力(ネット) ps/rpm	120/6500
最大トルク kg-m/rpm	14.0/5500
燃料供給装置	EGI
燃料および タンク容量 ℓ	無鉛レギュラーガソリン・45
駆動装置	
クラッチ形式	乾燥単板ダイヤフラム式
変速比 第1速	3.136
第2速	1.888
第3速	1.330
第4速	1.000
第5速	0.814
後退	3.758
減速比	4.300
操向装置	
ギア形式	ラック&ピニオン
倍力装置形式	エンジン回転数感応型 ※2
サスペンション	
サスペンション・前後	ダブルウイッシュボーン式
ショックアブソーバー・前後	筒型複動式
スタビライザー・前後	トーションバー式
制動装置	
ブレーキ形式・前	ベンチレーティッドディスク
ブレーキ形式・後	ソリッドディスク
倍力装置形式	8インチ径真空倍力式
タイヤ&ホイール	
タイヤ・前後	185/60R14 82H
ホイール・前後	5.5-JJ×14

()内はディタッチャブルハードトップ装着車の数値 ※1 スペシャルパッケージ装着車は10kg増 ※2 スペシャルパッケージ装着車 ■道路運送車両法による新型車届出書数値■燃料消費は定められた条件のもとでの値です。実際の気象・道路・車両・運転・整備などの条件により燃料消費率が異なってきます。■エンジン出力表示には、ネット値とグロス値があります。■「ネット」とはエンジンを車両に搭載した状態と同条件で測定したものであり、「グロス」とはエンジン単体で測定したものです。同じエンジンで測定した場合、「ネット」は「グロス」よりもガソリン乗用車で約15%程度低い値(自工会調べ)となっています。■付属品:スペアタイヤ・標準工具一式 ■撮影、印刷条件などによりボディカラー及び内装色が実車とちがって見えることがあります。■本仕様は予告なく変更することがあります。

主要装備

■エクステリア
リトラクタブルハロゲンヘッドランプ
フロント安全合わせガラス
フィン付ワイパーブレード(運転席)
ハイマウントストップランプ
ロッカーパネルピッチ塗装
カラードドアミラー ※3
コンバーチブルトップ
■インテリア
ウレタン製ステアリング
間欠式ワイパー
防眩式ルームミラー
AM/FM電子チューナー
カセットデッキ
オーディオ ドアスピーカー×2
　　ヘッドレストスピーカー×4
脱着式ロッドアンテナ
ルームランプ
キー付グローブボックス
キー付コンソールボックス
フューエルリッドオープナー
照明付アッシュトレイ
フットレスト(運転席)
テンションリデューサー付ELR3点式シートベルト
シートバックポケット(助手席)
ループパイルカーペット
4段階調整式空調ファンスイッチ
サイドデミスター
■メカニズム
フロントベンチレーティッドディスクブレーキ
リアソリッドディスクブレーキ
スタビライザー(前・後)
ビスカスLSD
■タイヤ&ホイール
185/60R14 82Hスチールラジアルタイヤ
5.5-JJ×14スチールホイール
センターミニキャップ

※3:フェンダーミラー装着車も設定
□速度警報装置はショップオプション

オプション

スペシャルパッケージ					
パワーステアリング パワーウインドー 本革製ステアリング(MOMO) 5.5-JJ×14アルミホイール	●	●	●	●	
CDプレーヤー				●	
ディタッチャブルハードトップ(ブラック)			●		
ディタッチャブルハードトップ(レッド)					
ハードスキット					
シリンダーヘッドカバー(メッキ)					
ハイテンションコード(レッド)					

B6・1600DOHCエンジン性能曲線

走行性能曲線

ボディカラー (内装色:ブラック)

クラシックレッド

マリナーブルー

クリスタルホワイト

シルバーストーンメタリック

---

launch, *Modern Motor* named the car in its 'Best Car Awards for 89/90.' The MX-5 scored 257 points out of a possible 470 to easily take the title.

Reaction in New Zealand was also favourable. In fact, *New Zealand Car* actually bought an MX-5, citing its good points as 'just about everything.' However, with a distinct shortage of supply and strong demand, many were being bought brand new on the 'second-hand' market, with as much as a 30 per cent premium - tempting people to sell as soon as their new car arrived!

The model's first taste of competition came in the Teddy Yip Race of Champions. The MX-5 event was staged as part of the 1989 Macau Grand Prix weekend and comprised 16 MX-5s driven by some of the greatest names in motor racing's past and present. Ironically, it was a Toyota Group C driver, Geoff Lees, who took the flag at the finish, narrowly beating Andy Rouse.

The new car in Europe

The MX-5 was making headlines in Europe, too. Writing for *Supercar Classics* in late-1989, Mark Gillies said: 'When the Mazda MX-5 hits the showrooms, it should offer all of the [original Lotus] Elan's virtues allied to high [Japanese] build quality, modern [but similar] appearance, far greater refinement and rather more crash protection.'

Even *Classic Cars* magazine was enthusiastic: 'Here it is! A new popular sportscar for the Nineties: the Japanese Mazda MX-5 combines modern engineering with the nostalgic spirit of Sixties sportscar motoring, and it costs about the same in real terms as an MGB once did ... At £14,249 we have no doubt there will be a queue of prospective owners chasing the 2500 MX-5s destined for the UK market in 1990.'

The enthusiast's dream realised.

The sports car is back!
The new Mazda MX-5 is all set to become the experience of the 1990s, offering the ultimate in open-top driving; wind in the face and the nimble feel of a taut and eager roadster.

Designed with classic looks and superb performance, the MX-5 has already caught the imagination and won the admiration of enthusiasts throughout the world.

Its lightweight body, front engine and rear-wheel drive configuration, provide perfect balance and handling mixing nostalgia with the modern; it is an opportunity to again discover the pure joy and passion of driving.

Some of the world's top motoring publications have already described the Mazda MX-5 as:

"Nimble, precise, even, smooth - wonderful" – *Autoweek*

"With 1960s style allied to 1990s sophistication and reliability, the MX-5 looks like a winner" - *Autocar & Motor*

"Just born and already a star" - *Road & Track*

"We felt like cheering" – *Car & Driver*

From the very outset, the Mazda designers' aim was to produce a sports car that embodied the traditional spirit of the two-seater roadster of old. The result is a car that instantly evokes a feeling of sheer exhilaration with one objective in mind - pure fun!

A classic formula
The MX-5 has superb handling and performance that has been internationally acclaimed. With its engine situated behind the front axle line coupled to rear-wheel drive, it has near perfect 50:50 balance offering the ultimate in road-holding, handling and ride.

The traditional layout of the MX-5 reflects Mazda's belief that a superb sports car has to have superb balance. To obtain the ultimate in handling a number of components have been specially crafted to be as light as possible; for example the bonnet is made from aluminium and lightweight materials are used for the bumpers.

This all means the car weighs only 955 kilograms, enabling it to be a sparkling performer, but for all its sports car attributes the MX-5 is also exceptionally safe. Its all steel bodyshell is immensely strong and designed for total passenger safety.

The MX-5 is a vehicle with a singular purpose - to be a sports car. Its classic styling, superb handling and performance have all been obtained without compromising comfort and space. In fact there is room

50:50
to accommodate two adults and their luggage.

The thrill is back
The entire concept behind the MX-5 is simplicity combined with fun. The styling alone reflects this thought; smooth flowing contours that provide maximum aerodynamic efficiency, yet embody the thrill of the classic two-seater sports car.

Its snug, low-slung cockpit has a distinctly traditional look and feel, with a leather-trimmed steering-wheel, large round instrument dials and high bucket seats. Once you're behind the wheel you will find out why it is just so special.

For a start, the gear change is second to none. Its short gear shift is more reminiscent of a racing car gear change than a road car. And the pedals have been ideally spaced to give both a relaxed drive and a fast gear change.

The Mazda MX-5 is putting excitement back into motoring.

The MX-5 is a natural competitor with its well-balanced chassis, high-revving engine and close-ratio gearbox. Models specially modified for racing are appearing on circuits around the world.

The folding hood is crafted from the finest fabrics and is effectively weather sealed throughout. It looks sharp, offers little drag and is absolutely unflappable.

In the interest of balance and weight saving, the battery found a home in a corner of the boot. It's compact, weighs only 9kg yet provides 32 ampere-hours of capacity.

Part of the first British catalogue for the MX-5, printed in March 1990: "The enthusiast's dream realised."

But the author was a little more sceptical, predicting that the new Mazda was going to find life harder in Britain than it had in the States and Japan. This country has always been extremely slow in warming to the qualities of Japanese cars ...

As I wrote in my second volume on the Nissan Z-cars: 'At the end of the day, British buyers want a badge, and often pass judgement on a car before they've even seen it, let alone driven it. They also have an image of pricing relative to the marque. If it has the right badge, it's brilliant and excellent value for money - the wrong badge, it's an over-priced heap of junk! In that respect, it is sad to reflect on how little things have changed since the early-1970s.'

British taxes on new and imported cars, which seem extortionate compared to America and Japan (and even some other parts of Europe), would negate much of the MX-5's price advantage - a Panther Kallista or four-cylinder Morgan could be had for similar money. The new Elan was expected to cost less than £20,000 (it eventually went on sale at £17,850), a TVR S2 was £16,645, the top-of-the-range Caterham was only £11,570, and the new Reliant Scimitar range started at under £10,000. Besides, the British weather makes everyday use of convertibles doubtful, and many would regard the Mazda as a cheeky impersonator.

In addition, if one could only use a drophead for occasional use, why not buy a real old English sports car? The classic car boom was at its height, so spares were plentiful thanks to firms reproducing them, and magazines were packed full of cars for sale. A monthly from the time of the MX-5 launch was advertising a chrome bumper MGB Roadster, fully restored to 'outstanding condition' for £9250, while a garage had a Lotus Elan S3 Drophead for

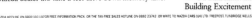
Early advertising from the UK. It had much the same theme as that in the States, harking back to the Sixties - a golden era for sporting machines.

£14,000. Both would attract cheaper classic insurance.

There was also the new Lotus Elan hovering in the background and naturally it took a lot of the limelight in the British press. However, in its guide to the 1989 Motorfair, *Autocar & Motor* said: 'Mazda throws down the gauntlet to Lotus as the MX-5 makes an appearance in the UK for the first time. Due to go on sale here this February, the MX-5 will be a crowd-puller as a logical, cheaper rival to the Elan.'

The Mazda MX-5 was actually launched on the 14 March 1990 (starting with chassis JMZNA18B200100001). It had the familiar 1.6-litre twin-cam engine, which in UK spec developed 114bhp, and a five-speed gearbox. Features included power steering, 5.5J x 14 seven-spoke alloys, electric windows, a Momo leather-rimmed steering wheel, black cloth trim and a Clarion CRH60 radio/cassette unit. It was available in four basic colours: Classic Red, Crystal White, Mariner Blue and Silver Stone Metallic - the same options as those for the home market.

William Kimberley reviewed the car for the April 1990 edition of *MotorSport*, and said: 'Considering that the car will cost £14,249 inclusive of tax and VAT, it is strange that the door mirrors have to be hand-adjusted from the outside, that a clock is not included and that the aerial does not fold down but has to be unscrewed to remove it. The windows, though, are electrically operated.

These quibbles apart, the car itself is a charmer. The gearbox is superb, the engine responsive and the sheer *joie de vivre* of driving it exhilarating.'

After recording a top speed of 114mph and a 0-60 time of a fraction over nine seconds, *Autocar & Motor* was equally complimentary. It said: 'The MX-5 is a total success. Mazda's single-minded determination to provide fun has produced a car of the rarest quality. Above all else it is its ability to involve the driver intimately in its every reaction and response that makes it a joy to drive. Few others, at any price, can offer so much.'

The same magazine later carried out a test to find the best-handling car on sale in Britain. Gathering together ten sporting machines and a similar number of drivers (including ex-F1 man Jonathon Palmer), the MX-5 came away a clear winner. It scored 23 points, eight more than the Porsche 944 and 13 more than the third-placed Ford Sierra Cosworth 4x4.

All of Mazda's attention to detail had obviously paid off and the press loved the car, but this would all be for nothing if it didn't result in people going into Mazda dealerships (185 in the UK at that time) and parting with their money. Fortunately for Mazda, the author's scepticism was unfounded; the MX-5 seemed to create a new breed of enthusiast, one not deeply rooted in the classic car movement and only happy to wallow in nostalgia, but a breed that simply wanted the fun of an open car combined with trouble-free, reliable motoring.

The end of a perfect year

Hirai summed up the general feeling by saying: 'Some people thought this simple idea was stupid, but the original RX-7 concept has gone too far upmarket. This level is now vacant. We may not make a big profit with this, compared with cars like the 929. There might not be so many of these customers, but they have very strong feelings. It is like seeing your former lover 30 years later.'

By the end of 1989, the MX-5 had already picked up a large number of accolades. In the USA, *Auto Week* voted it "The Most Fun Car," while *Road & Track* classed it in its "World's Best Cars" listing - out of the top five it was second only to the Ferrari Testarossa. *Automotive News* called it the "Hit of the Year."

In its home country, *Sports Nippon News* hailed the Eunos Roadster as the "Best Sporty Car." Even *Autocar & Motor* in the UK voted it the "Best Sports Car" in its review of the 1990 models. As 1990 progressed, the awards came ever thicker and faster, and from all points of the globe. It is doubtful whether a single model has ever before received so much praise.

A rare shot of MX-5 production. The Mazda sportscar was produced almost exclusively in Hiroshima, although for a brief spell, during the boom of the early 1990s, it had been built at Hofu in the Yamaguchi Prefecture. Once demand subsided, production shifted back to the Hiroshima Plant Complex.

After such a universally warm reception it was obvious that the MX-5 was destined for success. The popularity of the little roadster took everyone by surprise, and by the end of 1990 over 140,000 had been built (cumulative production of all Mazda vehicles reached 25 million units at the same time). Forgetting the 12 produced in 1988 during the pilot build, this meant that, in just two years, the MX-5 had outsold the Alfa Romeo Spider by quite some margin, despite the car from Milan being introduced in 1966!

To the surprise of many, the Eunos wasn't awarded the Japanese Car of the Year title. However, the car that did - the Toyota Celsior (or Lexus LS400 outside Japan) - was an exceptional motor car and a worthy winner, considering the market sector it took by storm. The new Nissan Skyline was another stunner, especially in GT-R guise,

and took second place. The Eunos Roadster clinched third, which was quite an achievement given the competition - Nissan's 300ZX and Infiniti Q45 and the new Toyota MR2 included.

In July 1990 the V Special joined the line-up in Japan to celebrate the first anniversary of the Eunos Roadster. A variation on the Special Package model, a classic wood-rimmed three-spoke Nardi steering wheel dominated the driver's view, and the natural theme was extended to matching wooden gearknob and handbrake trim. A CD player was included as standard, as were polished treadplates with the "Roadster" logo. Finished in Neo Green with a tan interior (including the leather-trimmed seats) and hood cover, it was available with either manual or automatic transmission and priced at 2,122,000 and 2,162,000 yen respectively.

By the end of 1990, a further 25,226 Eunos Roadsters had been

オーセンティックな深い味わい、Vスペシャル。

心と合めく穏やかな「人馬一体感」とともに、落ち着きのあるオーセンティックな味わいを丹念に盛り合ました ユーノスロードスターのニューバージョン、"Vスペシャル"。深くつややかな色合いの専用ボディカラー、ネオグリーン。キャビンをより個性的に華やかに彩る専用カラー、タン。上品な風合いとしなやかな感触の専用本革シート、あたたかなグリップ感が心地よいナルディ社製のウッドステアリングホイール&5段マニュアルシフトノブ、根拠装備のCDデッキ、パワーステアリング、パワーウインドー、アルミホイール、さらには、インストルメンタルパネル上面に施したなめらかな感触の新技術プロテイン塗装、新時代のライトウェイトスポーツを、よりエンスージアスティックに楽しみたい。そんなドライバーの願いを叶えるユーノスロードスターVスペシャル。もうひとつの深い味わいがここにある。

V
SPECIAL

キャビンは、ドライバーとクルマの緻密な一体感をもたらすタイトな2シーター、ショートストロークの5段マニュアルシフトレバー、ヒール&トウが容易なペダル配置などとともに、ダイレクトな操作フィールを提供。4速オートマチック車は、エンジンの専用チューンなどにより、ダイレクトで俊敏なレスポンスを実現している。

EQUIPMENT
❶パワーステアリング ❷パワーウインドー ❸木製ステアリングホイール(NARDI) ❹木製マニュアルシフトノブ(NARDI)木製パーキングブレーキレバーグリップ ❺4段オートマチックトップ ❻本革製バケットシート ❼CDデッキ ❽ステンレス製スカッフプレート ❾5.5-J×14アルミホイール

OPTIONS
❶クロームメッキシリンダーヘッドカバー・ハイテンションコード(レッド) ❷ハードスキット ❸デタッチャブルハードトップ(ネオグリーン)

sold, taking the home market total to 34,533 units. In the meantime, the M2 project had been founded in Japan, which brought together a group of engineers and planners to develop MX-5 specials (see Chapter Five).

The MX-5 in Britain

The 1990 British Motor Show was held at the NEC, opening at the end of September. It saw the world debut of the Gissya concept car - a futuristic MPV that perhaps predicted the forthcoming trend for this type of vehicle. Sadly, it did detract somewhat from the MX-5's justifiable impact. Mind you, with a lengthy waiting list only just starting to reduce, it probably didn't need any more promotion.

In the following month a hardtop became available through the dealer network, having been announced a few weeks previ-ously. Made from glassfibre, it sported a lined interior, heated rear screen, courtesy light and through-flow ventilation. Priced at £1145, it was produced in conjunction with TWR (Tom Walkinshaw Racing) of Oxford, and was listed in Classic Red, Mariner Blue and Crystal White to match car body colours, or Black with a grained finish. There was also a trolley and cover available for owners to store the hardtop safely when not in use.

The official Mazda UK price list dated 5 September 1990 quoted £14,899 for the basic car, with metallic paint adding £175, and air conditioning (a rarely taken-up option in Britain), putting a further £1259 on the bill. At this time, the turbocharged RX-7 coupé was £22,599, while the Cabriolet was £24,999. The most expensive 323 was £13,279 with prices in that range starting at £8469, so the MX-5 was not exactly cheap.

Indeed, Roger Bell, writing for *Supercar Classics* at the time commented: 'Here is a forward-to-the-past ragtop roadster that epitomises what fun-car motoring is all about. Apart from its indifferent performance, the standard MX-5 is hard to fault dynamically. Explicit steering is so sharp, so accurate that it faithfully obeys commands as if by telepathy. Fingertip delicacy is rewarded with composed balance and precision, just as surely as clumsiness is punished by raggedness. It rewards the sympathetic driver with an intimacy that no other Japanese cars (and few European ones) possess. The neat hood (augmented now by an optional TWR-made hardtop) is even better than an Alfa Spider's. There's only one serious problem with the MX-5. It costs £14,250 [*sic:* the price was even higher than this] which is surely far too much.'

Mazda wasn't the only company to display the MX-5 at the 1990 Motor Show, as IAD had one on its stand alongside the new AC Ace. This photograph accompanied IAD's press release dated 20 August 1990.

The Japanese home market's V Special of July 1990. The automatic gearbox option (shown here labelled number 3) was introduced in Japan four months earlier. A polished cam cover, uprated suspension and detachable hardtop (in body colour) made up the options list.

The V Special was introduced on the home market to celebrate the first anniversary of the Eunos Roadster (Japan's name for the MX-5). Finished in Neo Green, it featured a tan leather interior and a host of extras.

Action from the final round of the 1990 Mazda MX-5 UK Cup, held at Silverstone. Patrick Watts (who was declared champion at the end of the series) is seen leading Mark Lemmer (runner-up in both the race and the series) and Robert Speak. A total of 27 competitors took part that year.

The MX-5 BBR Turbo. Although the badging was very discreet, with "BBR Turbo" being added at the end of the existing "Mazda MX-5" script on the tail (as well as the trailing edge of the front wings), the catalogue described it as 'The ultimate sportscar of the decade.' The optional wheels were by OZ Racing.

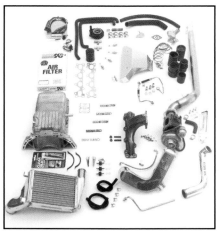

The various components that made up the BBR turbo conversion.

Nonetheless, by the end of the year Mazda UK had sold 27,598 vehicles, of which no less than 2246 were MX-5s. This was actually quite an impressive figure, for the rest of Europe only managed 7021 sales and Australia could do no better than 1446 units.

Inspired by the MX-5 race at the 1989 Macau Grand Prix, a one-make series was established in the UK. The 1990 Mazda MX-5 UK Cup was run over 12 rounds, taking in Britain's finest racing circuits along the way, with all the cars being slightly modified by Roger Dowson Engineering. Patrick Watts was declared champion after dominating the series; he finished on 116 points (32 ahead of his nearest rival). It is interesting to note that Watts was also champion of the Honda CRX one-make series that year, and when Mazda returned to the BTCC scene in 1992 (with the 323F), it was Watts who was chosen as its driver.

The MX-5 BBR Turbo

Although virtually all road test reports were complimentary, not everyone thought the MX-5 was faultless. In a *Classic & Sportscar* article comparing various sports-cars, Julian Balme pointed out a number of gripes: 'The God-awful positioning of the front number plate, the hideous wheels (if you're going to copy a Minilite, then do it properly), and the flip-up head-lights are like surfboards when erect. The other two things I dislike about the car are the steering and the lack of excitement emanating from the exhaust system.' To be fair, there were just as many things the writer did like, especially when he compared the MX-5 to his first generation Lotus Elan.

In the same article, Mike McCarthy had few criticisms, but in the depth of an English winter found that 'on slippery, icy surfaces, it was the most lethal of the lot, with zero grip. In any

direction.' When the final ratings were compiled, the order of merit was as follows: first, the AC Ace, then the Jaguar E-type, Alfa Romeo Spider, Lotus Elan, Mazda MX-5, Jaguar XK120, Chevrolet Corvette, MG TC, MGB, and finally the Fiat X1/9.

Once the honeymoon period was over, by far the most common complaint about the car in Britain was a shortage of horsepower. Mazda UK was quick to try and silence the critics though, and a press release issued on 8 November 1990 described a new turbocharged version of the MX-5. It stated that the latest model, known as the BBR Turbo, 'promises to be one of the most exciting sportscars of the decade.' The release continued: 'Mazda Cars (UK) Ltd, in conjuction with Brodie Brittain Racing, are proud to present the Mazda MX-5 BBR Turbo - a superbly designed sports package that retains the handling characteristics of the standard car.'

Brodie Brittain Racing of Brackley, Northamptonshire, is one of the country's leading specialists in the art of turbocharging, with years of experience in the field of motorsport. 'The Mazda MX-5 BBR Turbo can accelerate from 0-60mph in a blistering 6.8 seconds, and then onto a potential maximum top speed of 130mph. Even more impressive is the huge increase in engine power and torque performance - BBR has raised the standard 114bhp to a potent 150bhp, and torque has been increased from 100lb/ft at 5500rpm to 154lb/ft at 5500rpm - giving a massive 50 per cent boost in mid-range power. The result is that the Mazda MX-5 BBR Turbo can truly claim to be the new high performance sportscar of the 1990s.

'Yet for all of its attributes, the BBR Turbo is also one of the most tractable turbocharged cars available, whether you're motoring in town, cruising on the motorway, or just enjoying its handling and performance through the country lanes on a summer's evening.

'Priced at £2700 (depending on dealer location), the Mazda MX-5 BBR Turbo conversion is available from Mazda dealers throughout the country and is supported by a full three-year Mazda Cars (UK) Ltd warranty.'

The car was also offered with a special set of alloy wheels and Dunlop D40 M2 tyres (priced at £999.95), along with a limited-slip differential costing £620.98. However, Mazda was quick to point out that the package was more than just a case of bolting a turbocharger to the standard car - extensive testing in all conditions ensured that reliability and economy didn't suffer. In addition to closed circuit testing, more than

Another view of the MX-5 BBR Turbo. Like the other BBR pictures seen here, this press photograph was actually sent out by the Mazda UK Press Office, confirming the official status of the project.

	Standard MX-5	MX-5 BBR Turbo
Power	114bhp @ 6500rpm	150bhp @ 6500rpm
Torque	100lb/ft @ 5500rpm	154lb/ft @ 5550rpm
0-60mph	8.75 sec	6.8 sec
Top speed	121mph	130mph

6000 miles were covered on public roads, while the prototype turbo engine ran for 150 hours non-stop without missing a beat.

More than 140 separate parts were used in the BBR conversion, but naturally the most important component was the race-proven Garrett T25 turbocharger. A completely new exhaust manifold, cast in high-temperature alloy, and a stainless steel heat shield and exhaust downpipe were fabricated, along with an air-to-air intercooler. Competition-spec hoses were used throughout and the engine management programmes were recalibrated. In fact, BBR actually designed an auxiliary engine management computer to control the fuel-injection, ignition and boost pressure.

The figures comparing a

standard MX-5 to the BBR Turbo make interesting reading (see table).

After announcement of the BBR Turbo, *MotorSport* revealed that: 'The brief from Mazda UK was not an easy one, not least because the inside of the engine had to be left well alone. That meant keeping the 9.4:1 compression ratio, unusually high for a turbo engine, and also retaining the pistons, camshaft, etc. In fact, the conversion had to come in a kit form that could be sent to any one of 70 Mazda dealers ... To keep the Mazda warranty, 150bhp is the limit [but] BBR is working on what it describes as a Phase 2 conversion, that pushes out 230+bhp, although this comes without the Mazda sanction, and the work can only be done by BBR.'

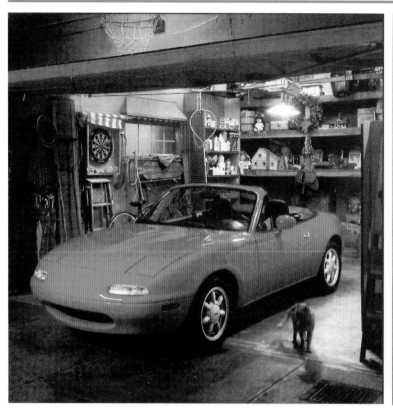

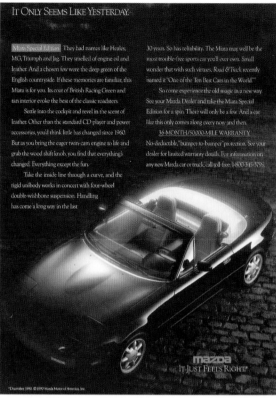

The attractive cover of the 1991 Model Year Miata brochure. The same picture was also used in magazine advertising in the States; indeed, through the years many Mazda catalogues have used retouched rather than new photographs to represent updates.

Tasteful advertising for the Miata Special Edition. Based on the Package B model, each car came with personalised interior badge.

The same magazine also road tested the car, and had this to say: 'There is little turbo lag and the engine retains its tractability. The delightful little MX-5 gearbox makes stirring the cogs about an absolute delight, but the engine has a broad enough spread of power to keep that a pleasure rather than a necessity. The 0-60 time is significantly reduced from 8.7 seconds to 6.8 seconds, and the top speed has become a genuine 130mph; a 130mph that in this diminutive, firmly sprung sports car is quite fast enough.

'BBR independently turned its attention to the suspension, and

in conjunction with Koni developed some dampers [shock absorbers] specifically for the MX-5. Some four or five combinations were tried before choosing the best. These [dampers] are combined with BBR springs that have a progressive action like rising rate suspension in motorcycles. The first portion of the suspension travel is soft, but the resistance of the springs increases as the deflection increases, so that in quick cornering there is far less roll than on the standard car, but the ride comfort is not unduly sacrificed. There are also anti-roll bars in the BBR kit.' Incidentally,

the BBR suspension kit was priced at £495 plus fitting.

An American update

During 1990, the Miata was named 'Automobile of the Year' by *Automobile* magazine. The car deposited with *Road & Track* had everyone in raptures although it was noted that whilst cold the engine had a tendency to hesitate and the brakes were a little sharp on the first few applications. Also, after just 9000 miles, the hood was starting to show signs of wear. However, there had been no unexpected bills, and only $70 worth of maintenance. Obviously,

American advertising from the latter half of 1991.

The 1991 Model Year Miata in Mariner Blue. Standard colours at this time included this shade, Classic Red, Crystal White and Silver Stone Metallic. There was also a limited run Special Edition in British Racing Green.

the title of 'most trouble-free' sportscar in the 1990 JD Power Survey was well-deserved.

Despite a poor year for Mazda as a whole in the States, Miata sales were still very strong in 1990, and it seems that *Road & Track* went a long way towards explaining why in a comparison test involving the RX-7, Nissan 300ZX, Porsche 944 and Toyota MR2. The magazine said: 'For most of us, the job of a sportscar is to take pavement - particularly winding pavement - and alchemize it into that elusive thing called fun. This the Miata does better than all the others ... A majority of the group said the Miata would be their first choice if they had to pick one car for the entire trip. A Feature Editor said, 'It has everything I want from a sportscar - it's fun, light, quick, agile and it's the cheapest. What more could you ask?'

Interestingly, *Motor Trend* had

found it hard to choose a winner when it compared the Miata to the second generation MR2 GT, declaring it an honourable draw, but in a similar test in the UK, *What Car?* thought the Toyota was best ... just! However, while only 25,000 MR2s were exported worldwide in 1990, American Miata sales for the year added up to 35,944 units - people were definitely voting with their wallets in favour of the Mazda. By this time, the changes for the 1991 Model Year had been announced.

For the 1991 season, the Miata started at $14,300, and was now available with ABS (Antilock Braking System) as a $900 option. One magazine stated: 'With that single addition, the Miata is just about perfect.' Maybe Mazda thought so too, for other than the new ABS system, mechanical specifications and options stayed pretty much the same as for the previous year.

However, March 1991 saw the launch of the high spec Special Edition. Basically - apart from a

few subtle differences (such as the steering wheel) - it was the American equivalent of the Japanese market V Special. Ironically, the dark green shade was known in the States as British Racing Green, but the Special Edition was undoubtedly an attractive package with its tan interior and hood cover, leather-trimmed seats, CD player, polished treadplates, electric windows, a personalised brass plaque and real wood detailing (including a Nardi gearknob) all coming as standard; a hardtop was available for $1400. Listed at a hefty $19,249, the automatic transmission option came slightly cheaper than usual, but demand for the BRG car pushed prices well above list in any case. In fact, all 4000 built were sold within just three months.

Looking at the bigger picture, demand waned slightly in 1991. But, considering the price increases and the fact that the Miata was old news by the end of the year, 31,240 sales - less than 15 per

A dramatic picture from the Japanese market catalogue of late 1991.

cent down on 1990's figures - was actually quite amazing. The Special Edition had obviously helped, but there was no denying that the Miata was still very popular.

The home market 1991

In July 1991, a minor change was announced. It was found that a 'performance bar' - basically a brace that connected the lower control arm pivot points on both sides - would stiffen the car and strengthen the rear suspension. Chassis NA6CE-150212, built in August, was the first car to receive this modification. Naturally, export models built after this date inherited the same bracing piece.

Sales of the revised cars began in August. The basic Eunos Roadster (now available in manual guise only) was still listed but was never particularly popular. With prices starting at 1,885,000 yen for the manual car (an automatic gearbox added 40,000 yen), the Special Package found a great deal more favour.

The V Special continued, albeit at a slightly higher price - the manual car was now listed at 2,157,000 yen, while the automatic came in at 2,197,000 yen. The Neo Green paintwork was still a feature, but the V Special could now also be bought in Brilliant Black (the first roadster on the home market to be offered with black coachwork). Polished kickplates around the door speakers were now a standard fitment on this model.

At the same time, Japan's first limited edition example was announced; the 1.6-litre J Limited finished in a colour known as Sunburst Yellow. Based on the Special Package, the manual car was priced at 1,900,000 yen, with the automatic being listed at 40,000 yen more. Features included the same Nardi steering wheel as used on the V Special, a Nardi gearknob (on manual cars), wood trim on the handbrake and stainless treadplates. A hardtop finished in the same colour as the body was listed as an option. The first J Limited carried the chassis number NA6CE-150211, and only 800 were ever built. Amazingly, they were all sold on the first day.

There was a rumour during this period, reported in Australia's *Modern Motor* magazine, that Mazda was testing a turbocharged 2-litre version of the MX-5. Given the lengthy lead times associated with magazines, it's unlikely this car had anything to do with the recently-formed M2 team, but mention was made of semi-retractable headlamps - a feature later found on a number of M2 prototypes. Whatever, nothing more was heard of the project.

For the 1992 Model Year, a side-impact bar was added to the specification (from chassis NA6CE-200000), and a remote bootlid release was placed alongside the fuel filler lever. A total of 63,434 MX-5s were built during the 1991 calendar year, taking the cumulative total to almost 205,000. Of these, 22,594 were sold on the home market.

Britain 1991

The MX-5 one-make series returned in 1991 (again, over 12 rounds), with sponsorship coming from Clarion, Car Line, Dunlop and Castrol. At the start of the year, David Palmer, Marketing Director of Mazda Cars (UK) Ltd,

said: 'The introduction of the Mazda MX-5 UK Cup has been tremendously successful. Throughout 1990 we saw some very close and entertaining racing at every round. With some new competitors involved for 1991, I think the series should be even more spectacular. It promises to be another memorable year.'

What Car? magazine voted the MX-5 "Sports Car of the Year 1991," further adding to the model's bulging trophy case. Then, on 14 March 1991, Mazda UK announced the £18,249 MX-5 Limited Edition to celebrate the first anniversary of the car in Britain. A total of 250 were made available, 25 of which were reserved for tax-free sales or personal exports. Another variation on the V Special theme, the British Racing Green paintwork was set off by contrasting tan leather seats and interior. Naturally, it came with a very high specification, and featured a wood-rimmed steering wheel, wooden gearknob and handbrake handle, unique 6.5J x 15 alloy wheels, central locking, four-speaker Clarion CRX111R radio/cassette,

Action from the third round of the 1991 Mazda MX-5 UK Cup. Robin Parsons (seen here leading the field into Druids) won the ten lap event at Brands Hatch.

The MX-5 Limited Edition.

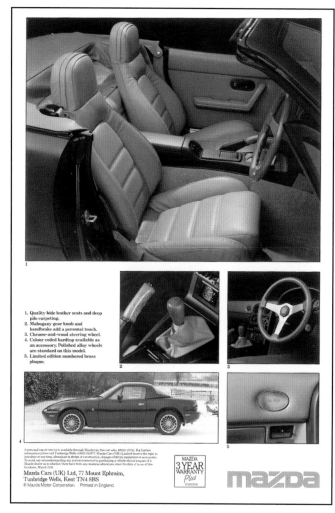

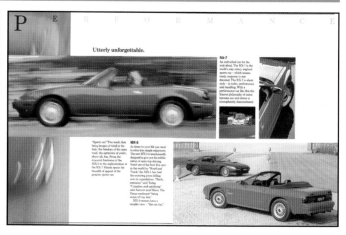

An English language brochure showing the MX-5 and RX-7; the latter in both closed coupé and Cabriolet forms. Although these are second generation RX-7s, the third generation was about to make its debut in Japan.

The sumptuous interior of the MX-5 Limited Edition finished in tan leather. Only 250 of these models were built and each was individually numbered.

Sadly, little exists in the way of official material for the MX-5 Le Mans. Fortunately, Paul Grogan took this shot of a car in original condition.

polished treadplates, a clock and leather-trimmed overmats.

The press release read: 'Each car will only be available in traditional British Racing Green and will come with a certificate of authenticity, stating that it is a Limited Edition MX-5, together with an individually numbered and engraved brass plaque mounted on the dashboard. To make each car even more personalised, a special leather owner's wallet bearing an identical plaque

to the one fitted to the car is included, along with a specially embossed leather key fob.'

David Palmer said: 'Following the successful launch of the Mazda MX-5 last year and the tremendous reception it received, we felt that a Limited Edition would be a suitable way of marking the first anniversary of the MX-5. Although this new version is mechanically the same as the standard car, it boasts an outstanding equipment list which

we believe makes it a very special car. We will only ever market 250 and anticipate that each one will fast become a collector's item.'

Following Mazda's success at Le Mans, Mazda UK launched the second limited edition model of the year. Writing for *MotorSport*, Simon Arron said: 'In celebration of the company's first-ever Le Mans victory this year, Mazda has built a limited edition eyesore. Looking like a cross between a stick of Blackpool rock and a jar of

Swarfega, the MX-5 Le Mans is equipped with BBR turbo kit (boosting power to 150bhp) and body addenda. It does not come with a free respray voucher, but that doesn't appear to have dissuaded potential customers, as all 24 have now been sold at £20,499 apiece.'

Obviously, Mr Arron wasn't too impressed with the colour scheme,which was essentially a facsimile of the bold designs found on the winning Mazda - bright green, and even brighter orange, in a chequered pattern. At least two have been resprayed black, whilst another was considerably toned down prior to sale.

The 1991 Earls Court Show saw the British debut of the MX-6. This elegant Grand Tourer (which eventually went on sale in the UK in February 1992) was joined on the Mazda stand by the recently-launched MX-3 coupé (known in Japan as the Eunos Presso), the top version being powered by the world's smallest V6 engine. The sporting theme was continued with the RX-7 Turbo Cabriolet and, of course, the MX-5, two of which were displayed. Apart from the usual 121, 323 and 626 models, the display was completed by the Mazdaspeed 787B which had won at Le Mans earlier in the year, and the Group A 323 rally car that Hannu Mikkola had campaigned during the 1991 WRC season.

At the end of 1991, Mazda UK calculated it had sold 22,416 vehicles during the year, of which 1986 were MX-5s. Although sales had fallen slightly compared to the previous year's figures, in actual fact, the MX-5 had taken a larger

1992 MAZDA MIATA ROADSTER

American advertising for the 1992 Model Year Miata, seen here in postcard form.

percentage of Mazda's market share, increasing from 8.1 per cent to 8.8 per cent. The 1991 annual sales total was the record as far as Europe was concerned; including the UK figures, more than 14,000 MX-5s were sold during the year.

1992 Stateside

Changes for the 1992 Model Year had been announced in October 1991. Of course, the suspension modifications which occurred in Japan in the summer of 1991 were inherited by the American cars, but more specifically for 1992 a remote bootlid release was fitted across the Miata range, and the Package B option now included an electric aerial; the optional hardtop at last came with heated rear screen.

In March 1992, the colour Silver Stone Metallic was discontinued and two new colours joined the line-up: Sunburst Yellow and Brilliant Black. The Sunburst Yellow shade was only available with the Package A upgrade,

although air conditioning, an automatic gearbox, limited-slip differential and hardtop could be bought as options. Like the J Limited in Japan, which was finished in the same bright colour, production was restricted, and just 1500 cars were allocated for the States.

The Brilliant Black model was not a limited edition but had a higher specification than the run-of-the-mill Miata. In fact, the black car was initially classed as a Package C option. Tan leather trim came as standard, and the hood was finished in the same colour to give a classy contrast with the coachwork. Alloy wheels by BBS, a Nardi wooden gearknob, wooden handbrake trim, stainless treadplates, cruise control, electric windows, electric aerial, a radio/cassette and headrest speakers took the price up to $17,500. Over 7000 were sold, prompting Mazda to rethink the Package C option for the 1993 range.

In March, *Road & Track*

A page from the Australian catalogue of February 1992, describing the MX-5 as 'The reincarnation of the classic sportscar.'

Another view of the model for the Australian market. Sales were strong in the Antipodes during 1989 and 1990, but dropped off rapidly thereafter.

carried out a test comparing ten of the best handling cars available in America at that time. Of the Sunburst Yellow Miata (complete with yellow hardtop), racer Danny Sullivan said: 'Well, it's a fun little car that's comfortable and easy to drive fast. The steering is responsive, but not too quick, and in the high-speed corners the Miata feels very stable. Braking is very good; I was getting deeper and deeper into each corner and I never sensed any fade. It puts the power down well, and you'd get a slightly tail-out attitude on the fast stuff, but it was not bad overall. It's a little underpowered, but that's to be expected.'

It was interesting comparing notes made by Roger Bell in the UK with those made by Danny Sullivan in the States. It reminded the author of a comment made by Maurice Ford, an old friend who used to race in the 1960s, regarding our mutual love of old Alfas. He said, 'You're never really going that fast, it just feels like you are!'

The MX-5 had been cleverly engineered to feel the same way. Relatively narrow tyres (at least by modern sportscar standards)

Interior of the Australian specification car. The handbrake retained this position on all cars for all markets, regardless of whether they were left- or right-hand drive.

combined with just enough power to excite, kept the limits low enough for people not to get into too much trouble - nothing will happen too quickly or suddenly as it might in a very high-powered machine, or one with wider, grippier rubber. While someone like Bell or Sullivan could extract the best from the vehicle, it was designed to flatter any driver.

In a *Motor Trend* survey, an amazing 97.7 per cent of owners thought the fun-to-drive capabili-

ties of the Miata were excellent; in fact, the car excelled in virtually every performance and creature comfort category, although it was perhaps significant that most people bought the car initially on the grounds of styling. With 17 per cent saying they desired more power, handling was highlighted as a specific area that most owners like and, with a fine reliability record, 73.6 per cent of owners said they would buy another.

All this press coverage and

The MX-5 SE of April 1992.

The MX-5 SE brochure showing salient points of the SE model.

MX-5 Special Equipment

When the Mazda MX-5 arrived in Britain it was unanimously acclaimed by the press and public alike for bringing sheer enjoyment back to the sports car scene. This classic two-seater, with stunning looks and matching performance, offers the ultimate in open-top motoring. And now it's been taken one step further with the introduction of the MX-5 Special Equipment Model.

Produced exclusively in brilliant black, the prestigious MX-5 SE is equipped with a rich selection of additional features, providing a rare opportunity for a privileged few to own and drive one of the most individual cars on the road today.

The refined elegance of the interior - trimmed in a luxurious tan colour leather, with deep pile carpeting, polished wooden steering wheel, engraved gear change lever knob and hand brake grip - is the last word in attention to detail. And as a finishing touch each leather key fob is personalised with the MX-5 SE logo. The potent simplicity of style in the MX-5 SE's external design is enhanced by polished alloy wheels fitted with low profile tyres.

The MX-5 Special Equipment is a car for the truely discerning purchaser. You should register your interest without delay.

The exterior is finished exclusively in Brilliant Black (PZ).

Interior decor is a contrasting tan with leather trim.

SE badging is the mark of distinction.

Anti-lock Braking System is standard.

Personalised leather key fob.

Polished scuff plates for sill protection.

Electric audio antenna.

Spoked 7.0JX 15 polished alloy wheels with security wheel nuts.

Low profile 215/45/ZR15 tyres.

Analogue clock.

Wood steering wheel *chrome spoked/wood rim wheel with an embossed leather horn push.*

Wood gear change lever knob *lacquered finish with engraved gear ratio.*

Wood handbrake grip *lacquered finish.*

Please note: Unless otherwise stated, specification is the same as that of the standard MX-5. All items listed as original equipment are fitted prior to vehicle delivery.

---

the special editions helped keep sales at a high level, and allowed Mazda to divert some of its advertising budget to other vehicles in the range. Of the 52,712 MX-5s built in 1992 (which represents a figure 30 per cent higher than yearly expectations declared at the launch), no less than 24,964 of them found homes in the States.

Although rarely seen in IMSA events, the Miata could often be found competing in SCCA (Sports Car Club of America) meetings. Indeed, the Miata took SCCA Showroom Stock C honours for the first time in 1992, this was a category ideally suited to the little Mazda.

The British market 1992

Features for the 1992 season included a remote bootlid release in the centre cubby box, security window etching, front number-plate holders and the use of a "Finish Line 540" radio/cassette in place of the Clarion-badged unit. Standard colours included shades of red, white, blue and silver.

Following the success of the previous Limited Edition model, Mazda UK decided to offer the MX-5 Special Equipment. As the press release declared, it was 'offered exclusively in black with a contrasting leather tan interior, together with a high specification list that includes anti-lock braking and an electric aerial. The MX-5 SE model goes on sale to the UK public on Monday 6 April and will be available throughout the Mazda Cars (UK) Ltd national dealer network priced at £17,788 (including car tax and VAT).'

Marketing Director David Palmer said: 'The Mazda MX-5 has proved to be a universally popular car throughout the world. In the UK we have launched a series of special edition models to cater for people who want to own an MX-5 that is a little different from the rest. We believe that the Mazda MX-5 SE will be another success for us. It has all the attributes of the standard car coupled to a very extensive equipment list.'

The Mazda MX-5 SE model was the first cosmetic upgrade to be offered in unlimited numbers in the British Isles, and featured Brilliant Black paintwork, tan leather seats and interior trim, a wood-rimmed steering wheel, wooden gearknob and handbrake handle, ABS braking, ten-spoke 7J x 15 polished alloys with locking wheelnuts, "SE" badging (next to the MX-5 badge on the top left-hand side of the rear panel), chrome treadplates, an electric aerial and an analogue clock.

In December 1992 Mazda announced the S Limited - a run of 1000 cars based on the S Special. Finished in Brilliant Black, it came with red leather interior, attractive gold-coloured BBS alloys and the Sensory Sound System.

Interestingly, it was one of the first UK models to be built in the Hofu plant, although production would return to Hiroshima by the end of the year.

Whilst reviewing the MX-5 SE in its September 1992 issue, *MotorSport* also mentioned that Lotus had stopped building the new Elan: 'Both received widespread press acclaim, but Japan's more cost-effective mass-production techniques have meant that the MX-5 is still being turned out - and sold - in high numbers, while the more expensive Lotus has recently been axed for financial reasons.'

Regarding the car itself, it was stated: 'Designed as a convertible from the outset, the MX-5 is devoid of the rattles and body flex that often beset cabriolets that have been adapted from coupé originals. Build quality is first-rate ... Whether or not one requires the SE pack is purely a question of taste and, perhaps, of budget. The bottom line is that the MX-5 remains a joy to drive, however you care to dress it up.' Mazda UK sold 1017 MX-5s in 1992.

The S Special and S Limited

Although the recession which followed the boom of the late-1980s hurt Japanese car manufacturers, it was a change in the local taxation laws and unfavourable exchange rates that did the real damage.

The exchange rates were holding Mazda back; a luxury car division (called Amati) was planned to compete with the Lexus, Infiniti and Acura organisations but, in view of the economic situation, the idea was binned. Yoshihiro Wada, Mazda's President since December 1991, didn't seem overly worried in public, although it came as no surprise that Ford's involvement with the company grew ever stronger.

However, Mazda was determined to celebrate in style the third anniversary of the Eunos Roadster and in July, announced the S Special. Production began in the following month so that it could take advantage of a scheduled minor change - side impact bars, and the option of an airbag (fitted in what for Japan was a unique four-spoke steering wheel, but was basically the same as the one found in the States) - and sales started in September.

The S Special was a distinctly sporty version of the Eunos Roadster. Available in Classic Red or Brilliant Black, it came with manual transmission only and was priced at 2,030,000 yen. It featured an uprated suspension with Bilstein shock absorbers, a front strut brace, 6J x 14 BBS alloy wheels fitted with 185/60 tyres, a Nardi three-spoke leather-rimmed steering wheel, Nardi leather gearknob, stainless treadplates and speaker grilles and a rear spoiler. The only luxury item was the optional Mazda Sensory Sound System - a complicated Pioneer 130w stereo system that included a CD player - which was priced at 220,000 yen.

In December 1992 Mazda announced the S Limited - a run of 1000 cars based on the S Special. Sales began in January 1993 (the first car was chassis NA6CE-209203), with the price set at 2,350,000 yen. Finished in Brilliant Black, the model came with red leather interior, attractive gold-coloured BBS alloys and the Sensory Sound System.

All told, 18,657 Eunos Roadsters were sold in Japan during 1992 - almost three times as many as were sold in the whole of Europe. Incidentally, the 250,000th MX-5 (built at Hiroshima on 9 November 1992) went to Australia and is now an exhibit at the Australian National Motor Museum.

The US market 1993

For 1993, the car's suspension was refined to give 'improved ride qualities without sacrificing

Two pages from the 1993 Model Year Miata catalogue, complete with retouched photographs to show the new badging.

The Miata seen competing in SCCA racing, where it soon acquired an excellent reputation. It took the Showroom Stock C title on several occasions.

handling,' but the thing most people noticed was the new badge on the nose (necessitating the deletion of the "Mazda" decal on the front bumper (even though some retouched catalogue pictures left them on!) and the centre caps on the alloy wheel option. In addition, the steering wheel boss now had "SRS Airbag" in place of the previous "Mazda" script.

An AM/FM stereo radio/ cassette with integral digital clock became standard, having previously been part of the Package A option, and Brilliant Black was added as a standard colour. Mazda's Sensory Sound System (MSSS) could be bought as a separate option, as could ABS braking (with Package B or C), automatic transmission, a limited-slip differential for manual cars, a hardtop and air conditioning.

Some of the cars on display at the 1992 Motor Show held at the NEC in Birmingham. Nearest the camera and to the left is the Xedos 6, while the new third generation RX-7 can be seen next to it. A 626 is behind the RX-7 and the elegant MX-6 makes up the foursome.

The MX-5 SE of May 1993.

A 1993 MX-5 in standard UK trim, just before European models adopted the new corporate badge on the nose and centre caps on the wheels.

The option packages were rearranged for the 1993 Model Year and included the following items: Option Package A added power-assisted steering, a leather-wrapped steering wheel, electrically-adjustable mirrors, alloy wheels and headrest speakers to the basic model. Package B included everything in Package A, plus cruise control, electric windows and an automatic electric aerial. Package C had all the items in Package B, plus a tan-coloured interior with leather seat facings and a tan vinyl top. This was available on all paintwork options with the exception of cars finished in Mariner Blue, which could be supplied with standard black trim only.

Midway through the year the Miata Limited Edition made its entrance. The American cousin of the S Limited, it was finished in Brilliant Black with a red leather interior (a red vinyl tonneau cover was also included), and included the usual luxury touches - a leather-rimmed steering wheel, a Nardi leather gearknob, the MSSS stereo system, stainless treadplates and speaker grilles, a special key fob and even a Miata book. However, ABS, a limited-slip differential, BBS alloy wheels fitted with 185/60 R14 tyres, an uprated suspension with Bilstein shock absorbers and front and rear spoilers were also included in the $22,000 list price. Only 1500 examples were ever built but, as *Sports Car International* pointed out, with the horsepower un-changed 'the engine is not enough to warrant such a harsh suspen-sion.'

Patrick Watts with the Xedos 6 developed by RD Motorsport for the 1993 BTCC season. Watts, who won the 1990 Mazda MX-5 UK Cup, had driven a 2-litre 323F in the previous year, but with little success. During 1993 he claimed the fastest lap on one occasion, along with a pole position. David Leslie drove the Xedos 6 in 1994 but Mazda finished the season early, pulling out from the series in July.

Dashboard of the French 1993 Model Year MX-5. Most pictures used in catalogues were the same throughout Europe (including the UK), and were simply reversed and retouched as necessary for left- and right-hand drive cars. Only the dashboard shots had to be specially taken. For the 1995 Model Year worldwide, the traditional style calibrations on the oil pressure gauge were replaced by "idiot-proof" "L" and "H" marking at each extremity.

The Miata was SCCA Showroom Stock C class winner again although it wasn't the only car in the Mazda range to acquire an important title; the new RX-7 received the 1993 "Import Car of the Year" award from *Motor Trend* magazine.

Sales in America were still falling but 21,588 units was more than respectable. Across the border, Canada took another 1501. Together, this accounted for the bulk of exports during the year as European sales fell to an all-time low.

1993 Model Year Britain

The Mazda stand at the 1992 Motor Show (held at the NEC between 24 October and 1 November), had the new RX-7 as its star attraction. As the press release stated: 'One of the highlights of the stand will be the Mazda RX-7 Turbo. This stunning new sportscar created a sensation at its international debut in Tokyo at the end of 1991. The RX-7 has just gone on sale in the UK, but with just 120 cars available this year, it is set to be be a very exclusive sportscar.'

Known in Japan as the Anfini RX-7 (and sold through the Anfini sales channel established in 1991), the 237bhp machine was capable of covering 0-60 in just 5.3 seconds, before powering on towards a top speed of 150mph.

The RX-7 joined a distinctly sporting line-up, including the MX-3, MX-5 and MX-6, as well as the 323, 626, and luxury Xedos 6 range. To reinforce Mazda's sporty image, the 323F used by Patrick Watts in the 1992 British Touring Car Championship was also on display.

From 4 January 1993, a number of Mazdas were subjected to price increases. The Mazda MX-3 1.8i now cost £15,729, the standard MX-5 was £15,780 and the MX-6 started at £18,519. However, the recently-launched RX-7 remained at £32,536.

On 5 May Mazda UK announced the second MX-5 SE. This latest MX-5 SE was basically the same as the original, although the alloy wheels were different on this edition (6.5J x 15), and the stereo unit was also changed. The press release noted: 'A new 1993 special version of the Mazda MX-5 will go on sale on Tuesday 1 June, available only in Brilliant Black with an extensive standard equipment list.

'The Mazda MX-5 SE, priced at £18,686, is offered in black and comes with contrasting tan leather interior with extensive use of wooden mahogany trim. The specification list is impressive and includes an anti-lock braking system, electrical aerial and seven-spoke chrome plated alloy wheels.'

Jan Smith, the new Marketing Director of Mazda UK, said: 'The Mazda MX-5 has proved to be one of the most successful and sought-after cars currently available. The fact that production worldwide has now exceeded 250,000 speaks volumes for the popularity and attraction of the car ... The 1993 Mazda MX-5 SE owners can be sure that they will be driving a very exclusive car indeed.'

By July a number of changes had started to filter through for the next season. On the safety front, the MX-5 now came with side-impact door protection beams; an electric aerial was declared standard, as was the Clarion CRX52 radio/cassette unit. The new corporate chrome badge appeared on the nose, replacing the old "Mazda" decal applied to the lower left-hand side of the bumper; this is a handy identifying feature when trying to date vehicles.

During 1993, Mazda UK sold a total of 18,944 vehicles, but only 910 of these were MX-5s - less than 5 per cent of Mazda's market share in the British Isles.

News from the Antipodes
After a high of 1446 sales in 1990, the Australian market was becoming something of a disap-pointment - 1991 saw only 746 sales and 1992's figures fell again to just 502 units. The press was still behind the car but it was the public that had to buy them. To try and make the Mazda convertible

The B6-ZE (RS) engine. It should be noted that on this 1.6-litre unit the maker's name and "DOHC 16-VALVE" is cast into the metal; soon, these would become a useful identifying feature.

more tempting, Mazda launched the $39,990 MX-5 Classic.

Finished in red with a tan leather interior, the package included BBS alloys, a CD player, a Nardi gearknob and handbrake trim, and even a signed picture of Toshihiko Hirai (he left the company shortly after to become a university lecturer). Limited to 100 units (this was Australia's second limited edition - the first was a Neo Green model restricted to 300 examples), it sold out almost immediately, despite competition from the vastly improved Ford Capri which was built in Australia and was some $11,000 cheaper. However, including the Classic, total Australian sales for 1993 still added up to only 453 cars.

All change in Japan
Kenichi Yamamoto, one of the main supporters of the LWS project, retired in early 1993. He had witnessed some enormous changes within Mazda and could be justifiably proud of the role he had played in the company's development.

Things were happening on the Eunos Roadster front as well. In February 1993, the V Special

adopted the Sensory Sound System as standard but, more importantly in July, Mazda announced the first major facelift of the MX-5. With Hirai declaring his wish to leave the company (he finally left in March 1993), Shiro Yoshioka was put in charge of this project.

Compliance with forthcoming regulations meant a sizeable weight-gain and Mazda decided the only way to keep the car's performance at its current level was to increase engine capacity. There was a possibility that the 1.6-litre unit would be retained and a new 2-litre unit introduced to augment it. Instead, the 1.8-litre BP-type engine from the Familia GT was chosen, largely because it was a good compromise: the 2-litre would have taken off some of the roadster's economical edge and meant higher insurance, while the 1.6 would have struggled to remain sporty with the heavier body when combined with an automatic transmission. Modified to give 130bhp at 6500rpm, the 1839cc unit was given the BP-ZE designation.

To meet new regulations the body was strengthened with a rear suspension brace ('Performance

それは、バランスの探究。

ユーノスロードスターならではの「人馬一体感」。その楽しさに満ちた世界が、いまあらたな進化を遂げた。目指したのは、運動性、安全性、快適性など、これからのライトウェイトスポーツが問うべき、すべての能力の高次元バランス。DOHCエンジンの排気量アップ、ボディとサスペンションの剛性アップ、さらに、ブレーキ性能のアップとオートマチックのリニューアル。すべては、ライトウェイトスポーツ本来の人馬一体感と、すぐれた危険回避能力に代表される安全性、そして、日常的な扱いやすさを同時に進化させるための施策である。新しいロードスターに託した開発陣の思い。それは、ステアリングを一度でも握れば、たちどころに知ることができる。

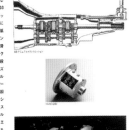

ユーノスロードスターは、あらたな自然吸気1800DOHCエンジンを搭載した。最高出力130ps／6500rpm（ネット※1）、最大トルク16.0kg-m／4500rpm。高速タイプのバルブタイミング、軽量コンロッド、新たに採用したホットワイヤー式のエアフロメーターをはじめとする吸気抵抗の軽減などにより、レッドゾーンまで一気に吹き上がる高回転性能とともに、ぶ厚い低中速トルクを獲得。ドライバーの意志にリニアに応えるアクセルレスポンスをさらに研ぎ澄ました。5段マニュアルトランスミッションには、確実で滑らかなギアシフトをサポートするため、セカンドにダブルコーンシンクロを搭載した。4速の電子制御式4段オートマチック「C-AT※1」は、よりスムーズな走行フィールを実現。パワー＆ノーマルモードを自動的に切り替えるオートパワー制御も備える。また、1／2／3速を任意に固定できるホールドモードと、ダイレクト＆シャープな走りを堪能するアクセルレスポンス。そして、トランスミッションとデフリミットに結合するアルミ製P.P.F.（パワー・プラント・フレーム）。エンジントルクのダイレクトな伝達とシフトフィールの高剛性化を実現する。FRのユーノスロードスターならではのアイテムだ。5段マニュアル車にはレスポンスにすぐれたトルク感応型リミテッド・リップデフ「トルセンLSD※1」（Torque Sensing Limited Slip Defferencial）を装備。オイルの拡散性を利用して差動を制限するビスカスLSDに対して、路輪のトルク差を感知しながら最適なトルク配分を行なうことで、安定したトラクションをよりダイレクトに得られる。これにより、アクセルワークで車体姿勢を積極的にコントロールすることも可能にしている。排気システムは、排気マニホールドからテールパイプに至るまですべてステンレスパイプ製。高周波音をカットし、抜けがよく低音のきいたエグゾーストサウンドとしている。

1800DOHCの冴え。

A double-page spread from the Japanese catalogue of August 1993 showing the new 1.8-litre engine (note the raised details on the cam covers), the Torsen differential and electronically-controlled automatic transmission.

SPECIAL PACKAGE
SILVER STONE METALLIC
CLASSIC RED
CHASTE WHITE
V-SPECIAL
V-SPECIAL TYPE-II
V-SPECIAL NEO GREEN
V-SPECIAL TYPE-II BRILLIANT BLACK
S-SPECIAL
BRILLIANT BLACK
LAGUNA BLUE METALLIC

The new 1993 1800 series in all its glory. Again, the Japanese home market range was very extensive.

Rods') in a U-shaped configuration, a cockpit brace bar joining the seat belt anchor towers and another suspension brace bar up front - all to enhance the car's torsional rigidity.

Suspension settings were revised to suit and brake discs increased in diameter from 235mm to 255mm at the front and 231mm to 251mm at the rear. A Torsen limited-slip differential came with the five-speed cars, and the optional alloy wheels were completely restyled. Interestingly, despite rim width increasing to 6J (from 5.5J), each wheel was around 1kg lighter than the original design, representing quite a saving overall.

Although the manual gearbox ratios were untouched, the final-drive ratio was changed from 4.3:1 to 4.1:1. The optional four-speed automatic transmission was now an electronically-controlled unit with slightly different ratios, but the final-drive was actually the same as the manual cars at 4.1:1 (instead of 4.444:1 as used on the automatic 1.6-litre cars), signifying another important change.

The 1.6-litre cars had carried the NA6CE chassis designation, whereas the new 1.8-litre models were identified by the NA8C code (production began in August on chassis NA8C-100016). A useful identifying feature at the rear of

The options available for the Eunos Roadster. Many of these items eventually found their way onto Japan's various limited edition models.

the car is that the script of the "Roadster" badge changed from black to red. Other distinguishing features included a different numberplate holder, standard rear mudflaps and the addition of large elasticated door pockets. On the base models, Classic Red, Silver Stone Metallic and Chaste White became the extent of the colour range, signifying the end of Crystal White and Mariner Blue.

Announced in July, 1.8 sales started in September. At 1,791,000 yen, the manual-only 1.8-litre

Series I standard model served as an entry-level Eunos Roadster, but the Special Package version (available with either manual or automatic transmission) again made up the bulk of sales. Weighing in at 990kg in manual form (10kg more than the basic car), it was priced at 1,966,000 yen, while the automatic gearbox added 30kg and 50,000 yen.

The V Special was continued (2,336,000 yen in manual form, or 2,386,000 yen with an automatic gearbox), but there was now also

the V Special Type II. The extra 100,000 yen needed to secure one added a highly-polished finish to the seven-spoke alloy wheels, chrome door mirrors and a tan-coloured soft-top.

The line-up was completed by the manual-only S Special priced at 2,111,000 yen. Based on the Special Package model, its colours were either Laguna Blue Metallic or Brilliant Black, and it featured an array of tempting items: uprated suspension with Bilstein shocks and thicker anti-

The J Limited II with its distinctive Sunburst Yellow coachwork. The wheels, being the latest seven-spoke design, were obviously different to the original J Limited, but the black windscreen surround was another useful distinguishing feature.

Interior of a late Eunos Roadster (this is a Special Package model) clearly showing the Momo steering wheel and cockpit brace bar fitted behind the seats.

roll bars; a front tower brace; rear body brace; 14 inch BBS alloy wheels; polished treadplates and kick plates (which surrounded the door speakers) and a Nardi steering wheel. Prices were around 36,000 yen less in Tokyo due to lower delivery charges.

A few months later in November, Mazda released a limited edition of just 40 cars finished in Brilliant Black with a tan hood. Known as the Tokyo Limited, this employed a number of interior parts used from the M2-1002 run (see Chapter Five). The cream leather trim was beautiful and the added detailing fully justified the 2,458,000 yen price tag - even the automatic version, at 2,508,000 yen, seemed cheap compared with the 3,000,000 asked for the M2-1002.

In December 'Mazda and Ford entered into a long-term strategic relationship to enhance their competitive strength,' according to the Mazda Yearbook, and in the same month another limited edition Eunos Roadster was announced - the J Limited II.

Based on the Special Package model, the J Limited II was finished in Sunburst Yellow, just like the original J Limited. However, the windscreen surround was finished in black on this occasion. The run was restricted to just 800 examples. Bucket seats with independent headrests were used, a CD player was a standard fitment, and Pirelli P700-Z tyres were mounted on the familiar 6J x 14 seven-spoke alloys. Prices started at 2,030,000 yen for the five-speed version, while the optional automatic transmission added 50,000 yen. Sales in Japan added up to a total of 16,789 units for the year.

1994 Model Year in Britain

Although the SE continued to be listed at £18,686 (its launch price), by now the cost of a standard 1.6i model had risen to a hefty £16,490. However, on 18 April, Mazda UK announced two new models - the MX-5 1.8i and 1.8iS.

The main difference to earlier models was obviously the increase in engine size to 1839cc, increasing power output from 114bhp to 130bhp and boosting the maximum torque output up to 112lb/ft. However, the new models also benefited from an uprated suspension and a stiffer body (through the use of the additional bracing described earlier) to give a better ride and improve handling. Inside, the old high-backed seats were replaced by a new type (like those found on the J Limited II) incorporating an adjustable headrest. Door armrests were deleted with door pockets taking their place.

The top 1.8iS model had all the previous 1.6i features but added ABS, a driver's-side airbag, new (and lighter) 6J x 14 seven-spoke alloy wheels, a rheostat for the panel lights, electric mirrors, an electric aerial and a Clarion CRX87R detachable radio/cassette unit.

The 1.8i was the basic model with 5.5J x 14 steel wheels, a urethane steering wheel and far lower level of equipment. The base model was sold without power

The true modern classic

The Mazda MX-5 first appeared in the UK in 1990 like a refreshing breeze from the past. Turning heads. Stirring passions. And persuading enthusiasts everywhere that in terms of sheer fun and exhilaration, there is still nothing to compare with an open top sports car.

The excitement the Mazda MX-5 generated is hardly surprising. For it embraced special values that many feared had vanished for good. And in doing so symbolises Mazda's uncompromised belief in what a sports car should be: affordable fun.

The original Mazda MX-5 concept was based on a single thought: that the ideal man/machine relationship should be similar

to that between a horse and rider; instinctive; immediate; tactile; moving together as one.

To maintain this driving enjoyment, every aspect of the new Mazda MX-5 1.8i and 1.8iS has been judged in terms of how it would enhance the driving experience. For this lightweight sports car, a front engine rear-wheel drive layout was still the natural choice and true to the sports car tradition, there's not an ounce of excess weight on either model.

Although the new Mazda MX-5 1.8i and 1.8iS models embody the classic formula for driving fun, there's nothing "retro" about the technology that has gone into them.

From the spirited 16 valve 1.8-litre fuel-injected DOHC engine to the ultra-rigid monocoque chassis, modern technology plays a major role. Enhancing safety and reliability. And making the driving experience all the more satisfying.

Wrapped in sensuous bodywork, and wearing a new style of ultra-light aluminium wheels, there's no mistaking the new Mazda MX-5 1.8iS for anything other than what it is: a purpose-built modern sports car that is designed to provide excitement from the moment you turn the key.

The traditional British climate doesn't put a damper on the fun. The strong weatherproof convertible top can be raised and secured quickly and easily by either driver or passenger.

The spirit of the classic lightweight sports car lives on in the new Mazda MX-5 1.8i and 1.8iS models, and continues to evolve in a natural way. There is no other car to challenge its claim as the true modern classic as it takes its place in the hearts of today's sports car enthusiasts everywhere.

Featured here in British racing green the new Mazda MX-5 1.8i entry level model.

The sleek profile of the new Mazda MX-5 1.8i model will appeal to sports car lovers everywhere.

Power to stir your emotions

From your first encounter, you'll remember the sound of the new Mazda MX-5 1800cc fuel-injected 16-valve DOHC engine.

This new engine unit provides quick throttle response thanks to a race-bred induction system, distributorless ignition, and a lightweight flywheel. Furthermore, it offers a smooth, linear power delivery all the way to the 6500rpm redline as well as ample low-to-mid-range torque. Pentroof combustion chambers and hollow camshafts are just a few of the technical

Torque curves that translate into smooth acceleration and linear power all the way to the vehicle's redline.

The 1800cc DOHC engine features electronic fuel injection and tuned stainless steel "headers".

enhancements concealed under the cross-flow aluminium cylinder head.

Helping the engine to breathe deeply is a tuned exhaust system with stainless steel "headers".

Harnessing the power of this spirited engine is a special 5-speed, close ratio manual transmission. The compact gear stick linkage has quick, easy movements to allow you to move through the gears with clockwork precision.

To lock the Mazda MX-5's drivetrain in rigid alignment, Mazda created an ingenious, aluminium structure called a Power Plant Frame (PPF). This is an evolutionary development of the classic front-engine rear-wheel drive layout, only used in the world's most exotic cars. During hard acceleration or braking, the PPF minimises vibration and driveline shudder and slack.

After driving the new Mazda MX-5 you'll never forget the way it feels.

* The Power Plant Frame (PPF) locks the engine, transmission, and differential into a single rigid unit to ensure a complete feeling of togetherness and a noticeable lack of drivetrain shock and vibration.

Safer for your peace of mind

Although Mazda intended to make the new Mazda MX-5 1.8i and 1.8iS models incredibly fun cars to drive, we didn't overlook the aspect of safety. In fact, we believe that safety features enhance driving pleasure by providing you and your passenger with greater peace of mind.

Exhaustive simulation tests were conducted in the event of a collision. Data collected was fed back to the body engineering group. In the end, they created a body that not only looks beautiful, but functions well if required to do so.

The same highly rigid structure that contributes to the excellent new Mazda MX-5 handling and steering response, also serves to protect the occupants. Stress-carrying members of the monocoque body were made as rigid as possible. The deep cross-sections of the side sills and the large central tunnel provide critical reinforcement around the cockpit. Even the floor panel is designed to function as a stress-bearing component. In the event of a collision, the force of impact is distributed through the

Impact-absorbing "crushable zones" combined with strong reinforcement around the cockpit to enhance occupant safety. (1.8i and 1.8iS).

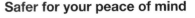

High-tensile steel side door beams provide added cockpit protection (1.8i and 1.8iS).

frame of the body and crushable front and rear sections of the car.

Energy-absorbing bumpers on both ends of the vehicle help minimise body deformation in the event of a front or rear collision. To provide an added measure of protection, the doors have been reinforced with high-tensile steel side door beams.

Flame retardant materials are used in the upholstery and trim. And the Mazda MX-5 1.8iS model standard equipment includes a full size driver's side SRS airbag.

Both the new Mazda MX-5 1.8i and 1.8iS models include a vehicle immobiliser system as standard equipment.

The new Mazda MX-5 standard immobiliser system is passive armed. To disarm before driving, touch the touch key against the dash mounted receptacle pad.

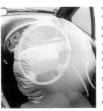

The new Mazda MX-5 1.8iS is equipped as standard with a full size driver SRS airbag that emerges from the centre of the steering wheel to cushion the driver's upper body in the event of a serious frontal collision.

steering, ABS, airbag, electric windows, internal bootlid release and radio/cassette unit. To keep insurance companies happy both models were fitted with an immobiliser as standard.

Going on sale from 2 May, Laguna Blue Metallic and Chaste White replaced the Mariner Blue and Crystal White shades, whilst British Racing Green and Brilliant Black became available as standard colour options. Classic Red and Silver Stone Metallic made up the six-colour range.

Complete Car tested a basic 1.8i in its August 1994 issue and gave the Design & Quality, Going & Stopping, Handling & Grip and Value & Economy categories four out of five stars each, with only Comfort & Equipment falling behind with three stars. After describing the car's original concept, it went on: 'As the years rolled by, a few changes began to detract from the concept. First, the car started to creep upmarket in trim levels and price. Then there was the compulsory catalytic converter, which robbed the engine of much of its pep.

'Mazda has corrected both these faults in the latest revision. The car now comes in two guises, with a cheaper, stripped-down version, tested here, for people who want to get back to basics. Unlike the pricier 1.8iS, the 1.8i has no power steering, no anti-lock brakes, no airbag, manual windows, steel wheels rather than alloys, and a plastic rather than leather steering wheel. But at £14,495, it's £2900 cheaper than the iS and around £2000 cheaper than the old 1.6.

'The engine has a low-speed urge that was never present on the 1.6, but it still has the rorty exhaust note that the company worked hard to achieve with the original car. It has perhaps lost a little of its smoothness at high revs, but it performs well - and smoothness is not the ultimate aim in this sort of machine. The gearbox still works with beautiful click-click precision and tiny movements ... The new MX-5 also has substantially better roadholding than the old model, particularly at the rear. The handling is better, too.'

Despite little change in the overall power-to-weight ratio, the magazine recorded a 0-60 time of 8.6 seconds, with a top speed of 119mph. During the test, 29.3mpg was returned overall, with 40.9mpg being possible at a steady 56mph.

In the same month, *MotorSport* tried the 1.8iS. It was noted: 'Until this spring, such changes as there had been were more cosmetic than technical. Now, however, the original 1.6 engine (which was actually quite perky, though made to sound more so by a trick exhaust) has been superseded by a 1.8 unit derived from that in the 323, albeit lightened. Power has accordingly risen by 15 per cent to 130bhp - on a par with the MX-5 UK Cup racers that provided the basis for a one-make series in 1990/91. The car is heavier, though (by 50 or 70kg, according to which model you choose), and doesn't feel substantially nippier. Indeed, top speed is little changed, at a claimed 123mph (up from 121), and 0-62mph will take an esti-

mated 8.6 seconds (another fractional gain).

'In parallel with engine development, the chassis has also been modified. Although the original was a paragon of balance and torsional rigidity, further bracing has been added, and the suspension has been tuned to cope with the extra weight. Mazda says that its intention was to "suppress roll during the initial stages of cornering and improve the overall ride comfort while maximising the handling."'

In September *Complete Car* published a comparison test. After the results came in, the MX-5 1.8i was declared 'The best all-rounder. This will suit the sportscar enthusiast just as much as the image-conscious looking for a fashion statement. It looks great and chic but is extremely enjoyable to drive, and still offers traditionally excellent Mazda build quality and generous warranty into the bargain. In this cheaper, stripped-down version, it is actually a pleasant change to find features such as manual window winders and steel wheels. This is the car which, at a push, could most easily be used as an only car.'

The £14,495 Mazda was awarded eight out of ten points, while the £16,600 Caterham 7 K-series took seven points. The Suzuki Cappuccino, the cheapest of the bunch at just over £12,000, got six, the same as the Reliant Scimitar Sabre which was slightly cheaper than the MX-5 at £13,995.

At the end of 1994, Mazda UK calculated that a total of 18,047 vehicles had been sold, 1250 of which were MX-5s. This was a vast

While the covers on the 1992 and 1993 issues had not been the most exciting, the cover of the 1994 Model Year Miata brochure was particularly attractive. The little Mazda entered the Guinness Book of Records in 1994 when the Miata Club of America managed to get 242 cars running together at Indianapolis.

1994 Model Year Miata in White. America listed Classic Red, Laguna Blue Metallic, White and Brilliant Black for 1994; the tan leather trim that came with the Package C option was available on all four colours.

improvement on the previous year, but how long could it last?

Australia 1994

Interestingly, the December 1994 issue of the Australian *Wheels* magazine, which looked back on the staff's favourite cars of the year, said: 'How do you explain other manufacturers' reluctance to tackle the MX-5? [It] still holds the monopoly on user-friendly, two-seater sportscars - a fact weighing ever more heavily on its $40K price tag.'

In Australia, although it was a fraction more expensive than the Honda CRX, the MX-5 was cheaper than a Toyota MR2 and about the same as a front-wheel drive Celica. Australia had two 1.8-litre models - the standard MX-5 1.8 and the Clubman - but the competition, armed with convertibles from various corners of Europe, was preparing to muscle in on some of the Mazda's action.

America in 1994 and 1995

Of course, the biggest change for the 1994 Model Year (announced in October 1993), was the adoption of the 1.8-litre engine. In US guise power output was listed at 128bhp at 6500rpm (a gain of 12bhp), with maximum torque put at 110lb/ft. Not only was this an increase of 10lb/ft, it was also more usable, coming in 500rpm lower down the rev range than before.

The American market naturally gained all the body modifications to go with the 1.8-litre car (namely performance rods front and rear and a vinyl-covered brace bar connecting seatbelt

anchor towers), the Torsen differential and restyled alloys (both in the Package A option), uprated suspension and larger brakes all as introduced with the bigger-engined machine in Japan. In addition, for the US, dual airbags were made a standard fitment.

Mariner Blue was replaced with the new Laguna Blue Metallic shade, and the "Miata" script on the rear badge was now in red instead of black. At the start of the 1994 Model Year, the Miata's base price was just $16,450, but few cars were sold without one of the option packages.

The popular Package A, priced at $1710, included power steering, alloy wheels, a leather-rimmed steering wheel, electric door mirrors, headrest speakers and (with manual transmission) a Torsen differential. Package B had all the items in Package A plus cruise control, electric windows and an electric aerial. Package C came with everything in Package B plus tan leather interior and matching tan soft-top. Separate options included air conditioning (at $830), ABS brakes, the new electronically-controlled four-speed automatic gearbox, a body-coloured hardtop, the Mazda Sensory Sound System with CD player and floormats at just $65.

At the Chicago Auto Show, where the Mazda stand carried a couple of interesting alternative-fuel MX-5s brought over from Japan, two new special Miatas were announced - the M Edition and the R Package. The M Edition was a luxury Miata finished in Montego Blue Mica with a tan

The R Package. Although officially announced at the 1994 Chicago Show, its sporty specification had been mentioned in the 1994 Model Year catalogue.

'95 is going to be a great year for Merlot.

MAZDA MX-5 MIATA

The 1995.5 Model Year Miata M Edition, the second in the M Edition run. This particular version was finished in Merlot Mica, whereas the first series had been painted in Montego Blue Mica. The colour changed for each season.

leather interior and tan hood. Features included highly-polished seven-spoke alloys, a wooden gearknob and handbrake handle, electric windows and mirrors, central locking and a special key fob. Weighing in at 1073kg, it cost $21,675 - $4,250 more than the base model at that time.

The R Package option was available on the basic car, priced at $1500. Stiffer springs, bushings and harder shock absorbers from Bilstein gave the Miata R notably sharper handling, but a choppier ride. With its alloy wheels, Torsen limited-slip differential and front and rear spoilers, the R was a pure sportscar. Features such as power steering and ABS were not available - in fact, a stripe (designed by Mark Jordan and listed at $230) and air conditioning were the only options.

Car & Driver found the R quicker off the line, but more importantly it was much better in manoeuvrability and slalom tests. It also recorded 0.86g on the skidpan against 0.83 for the M Edition. The magazine summed up the R with the comment: 'The suspension glows on the track.'

Sales for 1994 were almost the same as they had been in 1993 - at 21,400 units, there was a shortfall of only 188 cars on the previous year. In competition, the Miata took the SCCA Showroom Stock C title for the third year in a row (incidentally, the new 1.8-litre cars were placed in the Showroom Stock D category).

For the 1995 Model Year, it was decided to combine Package A and B to create a new option known as the Popular Equipment Package; Package C became known

as the Leather Package, although the R Package (still for manual Miatas only) remained unchanged. The optional ABS braking system was now lighter than before, and Montego Blue Mica could be specified on all cars in the range unless they were fitted with the R Package.

Midway through 1995, Mazda introduced another special Miata M Edition. Finished in a striking Merlot Mica (a purple metallic shade), it was priced at $23,530. For that, the buyer got leather trim, 6J x 15 BBS alloys fitted with 195/55 tyres, ABS brakes, limited-slip differential, Nardi wooden gearknob and handbrake trim, polished treadplates, M Edition floormats, a CD player and unique badging. A nice touch was the M Edition key fob and lapel pin.

While sales in Canada were

The Japanese home market's RS Limited of 1994 which was restricted to just 500 examples.

The Mazdaspeed catalogue from mid-1995. A combination of the Mazdaspeed front spoiler and side skirts brought about a 7 per cent drop in drag. Note the rather hefty Mazdaspeed anti-draft device behind the seats, fitted in conjunction with a rollbar.

This is the G Limited which had a run of 1500 vehicles based on the M Package.

The S Special-based R Limited. Almost 900 were produced in blue, with the remainder being finished in white to bring the total to 1000 units.

down to three figures, American sales for 1995 remained fairly constant, with just over 20,000 units being recorded for the year (around 3500 of these were M Edition models).

Japan's Limited Editions

Having seen how successful short run cars with various unique features could be in the cause of promoting sales for very little outlay, Mazda announced the 500-off RS Limited in July 1994. With sales starting in September, the 2,215,000 yen RS Limited was based on the S Special and finished in Montego Blue Mica. Interesting features included a lightened

Although much of the photography had been seen before (and quite a lot of it was shared within Europe), at least each country had a unique mix and highlighted different features. From left to right we can see the UK, Dutch and German brochures from 1995. The German edition (printed in May) carried details on the 1.6-litre model, but the British and Dutch catalogues - although printed around the same time - left it out for the time being as it was not available until the end of the year. Occasionally, similar-looking brochures would appear in the Far East; Singapore listed the 1.8 with a five-speed manual or four-speed automatic transmission while, for a time, Hong Kong was only supplied with the automatic.

flywheel, a 4.3:1 final-drive ratio, Bridgestone Potenza RE010 tyres mounted on BBS 6J x 15 alloys, Recaro bucket seats, RS decals on the front wings and a Nardi leather-rimmed three-spoke steering wheel. However, despite Mazda's best efforts, sales fell again in Japan; 1994's total didn't pass the 11,000 mark.

Undeterred, sales of the M Package-based G Limited began in January 1995. Priced at just under 1,900,000 yen in manual guise (an automatic was available on this model), only 1500 were built and were finished in Satellite Blue Mica with a dark blue hood. Low-back-type bucket seats, like those used in the J Limited II, were employed, along with a new-style Momo leather-covered steering wheel, seven-spoke alloy wheels and an uprated sound system.

In the following month, the R Limited was introduced at

The California Limited Edition. Note the windscreen surround in body colour - the second version of the home market's J Limited had appeared with a black frame.

2,175,000 yen. Based on the S Special, the R Limited came in Satellite Blue Mica or Chaste White (of the 1000 built the blue shade accounted for 894 sales) with a red leather interior. Like the RS Limited, it featured a lightened flywheel, 4.3:1 final-drive, BBS alloys and Bridgestone Potenza

tyres, but this time had a wooden three-spoke Nardi steering wheel and gearknob, as well as wood trim on the handbrake lever.

By this time, as Brilliant Black had joined the basic colour line-up, buyers no longer had to have a limited edition or the V Special for the privilege of black coachwork.

Mazda MX-5

Gleneagles
Special Edition

Designed for the true connoisseur

The revered style and performance of the MX-5 has inspired Mazda to design and introduce the MX-5 Gleneagles special edition.

The world famous Gleneagles Hotel and Golf Club is steeped in tradition, prestige and quality. These are values in common with the MX-5.

In unique Montego Blue the MX-5 Gleneagles incorporates many special features; classic leather upholstery and steering wheel, wood effect console trim and the original Gleneagles tartan together with the famous eagle emblem.

Unique Gleneagles MX-5 special edition vehicle badging.

Luxury interior leather co-ordinating vinyl trim edged in Gleneagles

Single disc CD player with RDS-EON radio.

To further enhance the pleasure and security of driving the MX-5 Gleneagles, Mazda have equipped this vehicle with power assisted steering and a vehicle immobiliser.

Gleneagles tartan owner's wallet.

16" diameter alloy wheels with low profile tyres. A matching hard top is also available as an optional extra.

Classic leather upholstery, leather steering wheel and wood effect interior console trim.

Key equipment

mazda

Mazda Cars (UK) Limited, 77 Mount Ephraim, Tunbridge Wells, Kent TN4 8BS.

Mazda Cars (UK) Ltd reserve the right to alter any specifications without prior notice.

The luxurious British Gleneagles model was launched at the 1995 Earls Court Motor Show. One example was donated by Mazda UK to be raffled (a type of lottery), the proceeds from which would help send Scottish athletes to the 1996 Olympics.

It went on sale from January '95. In addition, the S Special could be bought in Chaste White, taking choice to three on that model.

Britain in 1995

On 14 March the California Limited Edition was launched at the Design Centre in London to celebrate the MX-5's fifth anniversary, although sales didn't start until 27 May. Based on the 1.8i model, all cars had Sunburst Yellow paintwork, powered steering, 7J x 15 five-spoke alloy wheels and a Clarion CRX601R radio/cassette unit. Only 300 of the £15,795 cars were made, all carrying a numbered plaque on the fascia and a 'California' badge mounted on the rear panel.

Ironically, with people complaining of a lack of power on the old 1.6-litre car, just as many campaigned for a return of the 1.6i, not least the marketing people at Mazda UK. Higher insurance rates and the escalation of list prices weren't exactly hurting sales (one would expect them to fall after an initial boom, and 1994's figures were actually an improvement on the previous two years), but the competition was starting to get its act together, particularly the Rover Group with its new MGF. A cheaper car in the line-up would certainly help the MX-5 maintain its market share.

On 12 April 1995, the 1.6i was re-introduced as the entry level model to complement the £14,495 1.8i and £17,395 1.8iS. The detuned 1598cc B6 engine produced just 88bhp but, being priced at £12,995, few complained. Naturally, the specification was pretty basic - 5.5J x 14 steel wheels, no power steering, manual windows, no radio/cassette and the suspension and body-bracing found on the 1.8 litre models was omitted.

Oddly, the brake discs were reduced in diameter by 20mm all-round compared to the 1.8-litre cars (the 1.6i's discs were brought back down to the original 235mm in diameter at the front and 231mm at the rear), and it was initially only available in three colours - Classic Red, Brilliant Black and Chaste White. However, an immobiliser was included as standard.

Shortly afterwards, *Complete Car* stated: 'Mazda has cut the price of its cheapest MX-5 by nearly £1500 in a bid to beat competition from the new MGF. The MX-5, the biggest-selling open sportscar in the world, is now available from £12,995 for the 1.6i - cheaper than the original MX-5 launched five years ago in Britain.

'Commenting on the launch of the Rover MGF, Mazda Cars UK boss David Heslop said he believed its arrival would expand the market for all sportscars. "We're biased, but we think the MX-5 is a prettier car," he added. "And our research shows that real enthusiasts like the traditional formula of front engine and rear-wheel drive."' It's interesting that, via a quality newspaper, this

sparring continued. Rover bosses knocked the MX-5 by saying it had no pedigree and therefore the MG was better.

The author was at the famous Sarthe track in 1991 and witnessed Mazda win the 24-hour race, in addition to achieving some excellent results in various forms of competition in the States. So many companies have established themselves with good results at Le Mans, and some are still selling cars on the back of this reputation to this day. At the time, I was not an MX-5 fan, but I couldn't help asking myself if the MG marque had ever won outright at Le Mans! The argument could go on forever, but there was no doubt that Mazda had a strong competitor in the MGF, which was due to be launched in August to coincide with the issue of the new registration letter.

In fact, despite all the column inches on the smaller-engined car, the 1.6i wasn't available until November (by which time it cost £500 more). Official figures on the 1.6i quoted 0-62mph in 10.6 seconds and a top speed of 109mph. In the meantime, in mid-1995 the 1.8iS received a restyled steering wheel (complete with airbag); in addition, another limited edition car was on its way.

At the 1995 Earls Court Motor Show, Mazda UK launched the 1.8-litre Gleneagles. Based on the 1.8i, the Gleneagles was finished in Montego Blue and, although the hood was black, it came with a hood cover in champagne to match the interior. Priced at £16,465, it had power-assisted steering, leather seats, attractive 15 inch

five-spoke alloys, a Momo leather-rimmed steering wheel with the Gleneagles emblem on the boss, a wood effect console, a CD player, Gleneagles tartan trim on the gearlever gaiter and, of course, special "Gleneagles" badging.

Mazda UK Ltd donated a Gleneagles model to the British Olympic Appeal to help send Scottish athletes to the 1996 Atlanta Olympics. It was hoped to raise £250,000 through the sale of lottery tickets - was this the most expensive MX-5 ever?

The November 1995 issue of *Complete Car* pitted the MX-5 1.8iS against the new Alfa Romeo Spider (eventually launched in the UK priced at £22,000), the £15,995 1.8-litre fuel-injected MGF and Fiat's Barchetta, priced at £13,995. Tony Dron, a classic car enthusiast and ex-BTCC Champion, noted that the MX-5 'looks a little dated now, but [it is] still a yardstick by which to judge these new sportscars.' His article went on: 'driven fast, the Mazda does not roll excessively: it turns into corners well, understeering mildly at normal speeds. Push it a little harder and it's quite easy to provoke a mild and easily controlled tail slide which requires simple throttle control. Overdo it and you might spin but it is relatively easy to drive the Mazda in this entertaining fashion.'

The Mazda was the lightest of the bunch (by over 40kg), but it was the slowest and only the Alfa was worse on overall fuel consumption. Despite a number of compliments for the Hiroshima-built machine, in the end it was placed third, the MG taking the

その楽しさは、アクセルを踏んだ瞬間、きっと誰にでも直感できる。

The 1800 Series II range in Japan and its leading features.

spoils with the Fiat runner-up.

In its September 1995 issue *Car & Driver* compared the MX-5 (it was in Italian spec) with the Alfa Romeo Spider and Fiat Barchetta on home ground. The general consensus was that the Mazda was starting to show its age against the Italian newcomers, 'but it's still a performer, and a beauty in profile.' Perhaps the competition was starting to catch up?

One thing the *Complete Car* article highlighted was how little the MX-5 weighed. The 1.6i was naturally the lightest car in the range, tipping the scales at just 965kg. The 1.8i was 25kg heavier, whilst the 1.8iS weighed just over a tonne (1018kg). All were extremely light by the day's standards.

By the end of the year, the changes for 1996 were already filtering through. Armrests came back in preference to the unpopular door pockets, instruments lost their chrome ring surrounds and the 1.8iS radio/cassette unit was changed. Laguna Blue was discontinued from the colour options, leaving Classic Red, British Racing Green, Silver Stone Metallic, Brilliant Black and Chaste White, although the green and silver shades were still not available on the 1.6i model.

Amazingly, MX-5 mania seemed to gather pace again. In 1995, Mazda UK sold 17,775 vehicles (only a few short of the total for 1994), but MX-5 sales almost doubled - no less than 2495 found homes during the year. These were the best results in the UK to date, although most other markets recorded a fall in sales.

More changes in Japan

August 1995 saw the introduction of the 133bhp Series II 1.8-litre engine. Although the BP-ZE (RS) designation was retained, the Series II version featured a 16-bit ECU (Electronic Control Unit) and a lightweight flywheel to let the engine rev more easily. The 4.3:1 final-drive ratio was brought back on five-speed cars (automatic models stayed at 4.1:1).

An airbag was now standard on all Roadsters, the original low-mounted interior lights were replaced by a single unit by the rearview mirror, the chrome dial surrounds were deleted, the sunvisors became a simple one-piece affair, door pockets were reduced in size (and not fitted on the basic car or those with the polished speaker surround plates), trim materials were changed, and the colour of the "Roadster" script found on the rear panel changed from red to green.

The wine red VR Limited Combination A. Just 700 of these S Special Type I-based cars were produced, and sales started in January 1996.

Finished in dark green, this is the VR Limited Combination B. The wheels were later adopted as standard on the 1998 Model Year UK specification 1.8iS.

August 1995 saw the introduction of the Series II cars, powered by an uprated version of the 1.8-litre engine that had been adopted across the range two years earlier. Note the new-style alloy wheels on this Japanese Special Package model introduced alongside the 1.8-litre power unit in 1993.

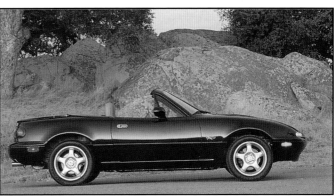

The 1996.5 Model Year Miata M Edition (the third in the series), finished in Starlight Mica. The first M Edition had been painted in Montego Blue Mica, while the second came in Merlot Mica.

Production of the Series II cars started on chassis NA8C-400007 and, as usual in Japan, the line-up was an extensive one. The standard model remained in manual guise only, becoming even more basic (even the hood cover was optional), but it was available in the full range of colours: Classic Red, Chaste White, Silver Stone Metallic, Brilliant Black and Neo Green.

The Special Package model remained the most popular, with prices starting at 1,930,000 yen for the manual or 1,980,000 yen for the automatic. The Special Package came with alloy wheels, powered-steering, Torsen differential (manual cars), a new stereo tuner/cassette player unit, electrically-adjustable door mirrors, electric windows and a new leather-rimmed three-spoke steering wheel, with airbag, of course.

In-between the base model and the Special Package there was now the 1,790,000 yen M Package. At 100,000 yen more than the basic Roadster, it had steel wheels and the basic three-spoke steering wheel, but featured power steering, electric windows and a decent stereo system.

The V Special grade was retained (starting at 2,300,000 yen), as was the V Special Type II with its unique features (again, it was 100,000 yen dearer). Colour options were restricted to just Brilliant Black, Neo Green and Chaste White on these models, and they came with a new three-spoke wood-rimmed steering wheel from the Nardi concern.

The manual-only S Special was also continued at 1,995,000 yen, but there was now an S Special Type II at 190,000 yen more. The extra money bought Potenza RE010 tyres mounted on

The Miata M Edition for the 1996.5 Model Year. The interior featured tan leather trim to give a tasteful contrast to the paintwork, along with wooden gearknob and handbrake garnish and a leather-wrapped steering wheel.

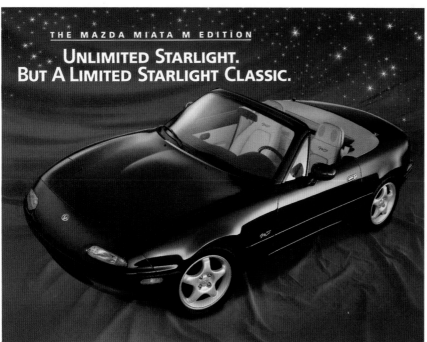

An advert for the home market VR Limited Combination A and Combination B models. The wheels were later adopted as standard on the UK spec 1998 Model Year 1.8iS.

6J x 15 BBS alloy wheels (the run-of-the-mill Type I had the usual 14 inch seven-spoke alloys, which Kijima said is the better combination). Incidentally, the S Special colours were Montego Blue Mica, Brilliant Black, Chaste White or Classic Red.

At the end of the year, Mazda announced the VR Limited Combination A and Combination B models; sales of these interesting variations started in January 1996. Both were based on the S Special Type I. The Combination A (priced at 2,080,000 yen and limited to 700 cars) was finished in wine red with a tan-coloured soft-top and matching leather-trimmed interior. An aluminium alloy gearknob, shift plate and handbrake lever were used for the first time. The Combination B was the same price

but limited to 800 examples and came in a shade known as Excellent Green Mica. This model had a dark green soft-top with black leather interior and the same alloy gearknob, shift plate and handbrake. Although based on the Type I, both cars had five-spoke 6J x 15 alloys instead of the familiar seven-spoke variety.

Despite the many changes in the range - and the special editions - sales continued to fall rapidly in Japan. In fact, only 7178 Mazda roadsters were sold on the home market during 1995. This meant that for the first time European sales figures exceeded those for Japan.

America in 1996

The 1996 Model Year changes were announced in October 1995.

Engine power increased to 133bhp, but the main concerns were meeting new regulations; namely, 1997 Federal side-impact requirements and OBD-II emissions. Other more minor changes included relocation of the interior lights and the addition of a small light in the boot; the MSSS was now known as the Mazda Premium Sound System.

The three option packages from 1995 were available again - the Popular Equipment Package, the Leather Package and the R Package, but there was now also a Power Steering Package that added just power-assisted steering and wheel trim rings to the basic car. Just four colours were listed as standard: Classic Red, Brilliant Black, White and Montego Blue

Mica. These colours were available across the range with the exception of the blue which couldn't be had with the R Package.

Midway through 1996, the Miata M Edition appeared in Starlight Mica, an attractive dark blue metallic shade found on the Millennia saloon. Trimmed in tan leather with a matching tan-coloured hood and hood cover, the high spec package included such niceties as five-spoke alloys fitted with 195/50 R15 tyres, Nardi wooden gearknob and handbrake trim and a leather-rimmed steering wheel. The only options were automatic transmission and a hardtop as virtually everything else seemed to be fitted anyway.

The USA took another 18,408 Miatas during 1996 (the M Edition accounted for 2968 of these). This meant the running total for American sales now stood at a massive 196,770 units, which represented 48 per cent of production at that time.

The Land of the Rising Sun in 1996

Mazda built a total of 1,197,872 vehicles in 1987, of which over two-thirds were passenger cars. Production figures rose to a peak of 1,422,624 in 1990 before falling back to just over one-million in 1993. Since then, production has continued to fall, with only 773,567 vehicles built in 1996 (around 600,000 were passenger cars and well over half of these were exported).

The MX-5 accounted for less than 1 per cent of this figure, but by the end of the year cumulative production of the MX-5 had

Introduced in December 1996 the B2 Limited was based on the M Package and restricted to 1000 examples. B2 stood for Blue & Bright.

Announced at the same time as the B2 Limited, the R2 Limited was based on the S Special Type I. With R2 standing for Racy & Red (the red referring to the car's interior), production was limited to only 500 units.

reached more than 400,000 units (the 400,000th vehicle was built on 2 December 1996). The RX-7 was approaching 795,000 at this time, although it had been in production since 1978, of course.

In 1996 Eunos sales outlets were integrated into the Mazda Anfini, Mazda or Ford sales outlets and the Eunos Roadster sold through the Mazda Anfini sales channel, lining up alongside the RX-7, MS8, MPV and Eunos Presso. The Anfini network boasted 87 dealerships with a total of 633 outlets across Japan, but annual sales figures were still dismal, with less than 5000 cars finding homes during the year.

At the end of 1996 in December, all models adopted a new Momo four-spoke steering wheel (with airbag) and two more limited edition Eunos Roadsters came

along: the B2 Limited at 1,898,000 yen (or 1,993,000 with automatic transmission) and the manual-only B2 Limited at 2,098,000 yen.

Based on the M Package, B2 apparently stood for Blue & Bright, although the Twilight Blue Mica shade chosen for the vehicle was hardly the brightest in the Mazda range and the black interior was rather austere to say the least. Anyway, limited to 1000 examples, the main features included a dark blue soft-top, highly-polished 14 inch seven-spoke alloys, chrome door mirrors, moquette-trimmed bucket seats, chromed dial surrounds and a combined CD/cassette/radio unit. Air conditioning was available as an option.

The 500-off R2 Limited - which was based on the S Special Type I - came in Chaste White, despite R2 standing for Racy &

Red! This designation actually referred to the red and black interior, which included red leather seats. Bridgestone Potenza tyres came on 6J x 15 five-spoke alloys, while the aluminium alloy gearknob, shift plate and hand-brake lever were revived and chromed dial surrounds as found on the B2 version used.

The British market in 1996

A Mazda UK press release described the salient features of the MX-5 as follows: 'The race-bred induction system, distributor-less ignition and lightweight flywheel ensure a quick, lively throttle response ... The drivetrain is locked in rigid alignment by means of an ingenious aluminium powerplant frame. Suspension is all-independent, using double-wishbones and anti-roll bars, while a brace bar and performance rods increase body rigidity on 1.8i models for enhanced chassis control.

'The rack-and-pinion steering has just 3.3 turns lock-to-lock and with power assistance on the 1.8iS this is reduced to 2.8. Braking is by discs all-round, ventilated at the front, solid at the back, and reinforced by ABS on the 1.8iS.

'For security all models are fitted with an engine immobiliser, security-coded window etching, lockable glovebox and central storage box and remote fuel flap releases.

'The plastic nose section is designed to resist stone chips and incorporates pop-up halogen headlamps. Everything is set up for a sporty experience: the tightly

A British spec 1.8i model in Classic Red dating from the early part of 1996. Other colours included Brilliant Black, Chaste White, Silver Stone Metallic and British Racing Green, although the last two mentioned were not available on the 1.6i. Note the standard steel wheels.

The 1.8iS model from the same year with alloy wheels as standard.

The Merlot (right) was launched in the UK in mid-1996 alongside the smaller-engined Monaco. It came with a luxurious grey leather trim, wood finish to the dashboard and a leather-rimmed steering wheel; a CD player also came as standard. Although both models had five-spoke alloy wheels, they were actually of a slightly different design.

MX-5

1.8 LTR LIMITED EDITION

- Neo Green
- Tan leather seats
- Tan soft top tonneau cover
- CD player and tweeter speakers

grouped pedals and dials, leather steering wheel on the 1.8iS, the driver's left-foot rest.

'But safety is built in too, from the side-impact door beams and energy-absorbing bumpers to the flame-retardant trim and upholstery. A driver's-side airbag and anti-lock braking are standard on the 1.8iS, which offers additional luxury with its detachable RDS radio/cassette, alloy wheels, electric windows and door mirrors and remote boot opening.'

On 12 June 1996, Mazda UK announced two new limited edition models: the MX-5 1.6 Monaco and the MX-5 1.8 Merlot. From the press release it was obvious that these were intended as direct competition for a certain Rover Group product: 'The Mazda MX-5 Monaco costs £13,750 - which is £2645 below the price of the cheapest MGF - while the high specification MX-5 Merlot costs nearly £2500 less than the MGF VVC at £16,350.

'Finished in British Racing Green and fitted with a tan hood, the Monaco is mechanically identical to the MX-5 1.6i. Special features of this limited edition roadster include alloy wheels and radio/cassette player. The MX-5 Monaco has a top speed of 109mph and accelerates from 0-62mph in 10.6 seconds. It achieves 42.2mpg at a steady 56mph.

'The luxurious Merlot - which has a special deep lustrous red body colour called Vin Rouge - has [light grey] leather upholstery, quality wood trim, a CD sound system, alloy wheels and power-assisted steering [along with a Momo leather-trimmed steering

Cover from the 1997 Model Year Miata catalogue. This was the last one produced for the first generation car as there was no 1998 Model Year car for the States.

The M Edition for 1997, the fourth in the series, was finished in Marina Green Mica. The first had been painted in Montego Blue Mica, while those that followed came in Merlot Mica and Starlight Mica respectively.

The well-equipped Miata STO Edition was announced in July 1997. STO stood for Special Touring Option.

wheel]. The 1.8-litre, 16v engine develops 131bhp to give acceleration from 0-62mph in 8.6 seconds, plus a top speed of 123mph. It returns more than 40mpg in the steady 56mph test.'

Although Australian sales picked up very slightly (241 units for the year, taking the running total for that country to 4609), Europe was the only market to show a notable improvement. In Britain, MX-5 sales continued to strengthen. During 1996, Mazda UK had a bumper year, selling no fewer than 3855 examples of the popular convertible. The European mainland recorded 5730 sales, bringing the total for the whole of Europe to a healthy 9585 - more than twice the figure for the home market during the same period!

The American scene 1997

In 1997 the MX-5 Miata was included by the American *Automo-*

bile magazine in the "All Stars" listing for its seventh consecutive year. 1997's colour schemes remained the same as the 1996 Model Year but the options were revised.

The Power Steering Package included power-assisted steering and wheel trim rings, while the new Touring Package listed power steering, a leather-wrapped steering wheel, electric windows, electrically-adjustable door mirrors, alloy wheels and door map pockets. The latest Popular Equipment Package had everything in the Touring Package, plus a Torsen lsd (for manual cars), the rear subframe performance rods, speakers in the headrests, cruise control and an electric aerial. The Leather Package built on the Popular Equipment Package with a tan leather interior and tan vinyl top. The R Package (for manual cars only) incorporated an uprated suspension with Bilstein shock absorbers, front and rear spoilers, a rear skirt, Torsen limited-slip differential, rear subframe performance rods and alloy wheels with locking wheelnuts.

The M Edition for the 1997 Model Year was dark green on this occasion, finished in a shade known as Marina Green Mica which was set off by the contrasting tan leather trim and hood. Other features included highly-polished six-spoke 15 inch alloy wheels, stainless treadplates, special floormats, Nardi wooden gearknob and handbrake trim, a CD player and air conditioning.

A press release dated 1 July described the latest American special edition - the $22,520 STO. It read: 'Arriving just in time to make the most of warm summer nights throughout the country, Mazda has announced the addition of a new limited-production version of the company's classic roadster - the 1997.5 MX-5 Miata STO Edition. The STO stands for Special Touring Option, a combination of popular options that embodies the true lightweight, affordable sportscar spirit of the Miata ... Only 1500 of the Miata STO Edition will be produced.

'Highlighting the 1997.5 STO Edition is Twilight Blue Mica paint, topped off by a tan leather interior and tan vinyl top. In addition to the unique paint scheme, the STO Edition features special Enkei 15 inch wheels and low-profile 50-series tyres; rear lip spoiler; STO Edition logos on the floormats; Nardi leather shift knob (manual transmission only); stainless steel scuff plates; an STO Edition sequentially numbered dash plaque, and certificate of authenticity.

'The car is also equipped with a full complement of luxury features, including headrest speakers, leather-wrapped steering wheel, power mirrors, power windows and a CD player. The only options are air conditioning and a four-speed automatic transmission.'

The situation in the UK

By this time the Mazda had acquired a whole string of competitors. The BMW Z3 was another newcomer (albeit a more expensive one), but comparing it to the MX-5, Gavin Conway of *Autocar* said: 'The Z3 has more cabin space, better performance, more mature yet still enjoyable handling and a much bigger dose of badge-pride.'

In January 1997 the Dakar Limited Edition was announced with just 400 cars made available. Finished in Twilight Blue Metallic, the interior came in mid-grey leather with dark blue piping. Other features included unique 15 inch 16-spoke alloy wheels, burr walnut trim, a chrome rear brace bar, chrome treadplates, a Momo leather steering wheel, Dakar floormats in grey with dark blue edging, a radio/cassette unit and power steering. Each vehicle had a numbered plaque and "Dakar" badging and an on-the-road price of £17,210 .

By the spring of 1997 a high-level brake light had found its way onto the bootlid; the interior light was now incorporated into a new rearview mirror and the 1.8i had the same boot release arrangement as on the 1.8iS.

On 16 May 1997 Mazda UK announced the special edition MX-5 Monza. Named after the famous Italian racing circuit, the Monza was finished in British Racing Green and priced at £14,595. Limited to just 800 examples, it featured 14 inch five-spoke alloy wheels with locking wheelnuts, an uprated sound system and exclusive Monza badging, in addition to the standard Mazda engine immobiliser and side-impact beams of the 1.6i upon which it was based.

A fortnight later on 29 May this was followed by the MX-5 Harvard. Based on the MX-5 1.8i in Silver Stone Metallic, it was equipped with power steering, 15

Typisch Sportwagen:
Die bequemen Schalensitze geben viel Seitenhalt

Funktionales Interieur:
So einfach hat ein Roadster innen auszusehen

Schöne Beine:
Spezial-Leichtmetallfelgen für die HE-Versionen

EINE HEISSE BEZIEHU[...]

*Da schlägt der Puls plötzlich höher: Die tie[...]
dem Asphalt, das schnörkellose Armaturen[...]
und das tolle Gefühl, in einem reinrassiger[...]
griffen ist das Verdeck geöffnet und Sonne [...]
Dreh am Zündschlüssel – was nun kommt,[...]
ultrakurzen Schaltknüppel reicht, um den [...]
Klacken einzurasten. Was für ein Getriebe[...]
Joystick lässt es sich blitzschnell schalten.*

*Ein sanfter Druck aufs Gaspedal
und der wendige Heck-
triebler spurtet agil von
Kurve zu Kurve. Man
wünscht sich, die Strasse
möge nie mehr enden. Die direkt ausge-
legte Lenkung überträgt jeden noch so kle[...]
nen Befehl äusserst präzise. Das Sportfahr[...]
an allen vier Rädern lässt Parallelen zu ei[...]
unser kleiner Renner basiert schliesslich ni[...]
auto, sondern wurde von Grund auf als R[...]
wir es vergessen: Der MX-5, so heisst das [...]
briolets, ist ein echter Sportsfreund geblieb[...]
Grossverdiener zu sein, um ihn fahren zu [...]
Mazda-like, das heisst spitzenmässig. Das [...]
über 300 000 glückliche MX-5-Besitzer in [...]*

Das abgebildete Modell HE verfügt in der Schweiz über Spezialfelgen (siehe Detailabbildung [...]

Part of the Swiss MX-5 catalogue dating from early 1997. Note the different five-spoke alloys available on the so-called HE version.

Unverwechselbares Gesicht:
Klappscheinwerfer prägen die markante Front

Einleuchtende Sache:
Dritte Bremsleuchte, integriert im Kofferraumdeckel

Eine starke Seite:
Aufprallschutz in den Türen ist selbstverständlich

on, nur eine Handbreit über
ssischen Rundinstrumenten
sitzen. Mit wenigen Hand-
das Interieur. Nur noch ein
rfreude. Ein Griff zum
ng mit einem satten
e mit einem

Gutes Gefühl:
So viel Spass, wie er macht, so zuverlässig ist er auch

pelten Dreieckquerlenkern
gen erkennen. Kein Wunder,
gewöhnlichen Grossserien-
ickelt. Ach ja, beinahe hätten
r den modernen Sportca-
ht man nicht unbedingt
d seine Zuverlässigkeit ist
ur wir, das sagen bereits weit

ZWEI ECHTE SPORTMOTOREN

Die klassische DOHC-Bauweise mit zwei obenliegenden
Nockenwellen und 16 Ventilen ist für die beiden Vier-
Zylinder-Motoren charakteristisch. Sowohl der 1,6-Liter
(66 kW/90 PS) als auch der 1,8-Liter (96 kW/130 PS)
wurden sorgfältig auf den Mazda MX-5 abgestimmt.
Um die Fahrt auch akustisch zum Vergnügen zu machen,
testeten die Mazda-Techniker unzählige Auspuffvarian-
ten, bis sie den optimalen Wirkungsgrad und die richtige
Tonlage gefunden haben. Die schönste Musik, um in 8,7
Sekunden von 0 auf 100 km/h zu beschleunigen – wenn's
denn unbedingt sein muss.

Der Ton macht die Musik:
Spritzige Sportmotoren beflügeln den MX-5

inch five-spoke alloy wheels, burgundy leather upholstery with grey piping, a CD player, immobiliser, chrome brace bar, wood trim, Momo leather-trimmed steering wheel, high-level stop lamp, locking wheelnuts, polished treadplates and special floormats with the Harvard logo.

The Harvard was priced at £17,495. To put this into perspective, the July price list quoted £14,410 for the 1.6i, the 1.8i was exactly £1000 more and the 1.8iS was £18,510. Mica and metallic paint finishes cost £250 extra, leather trim added £923 to the list price and air conditioning (available on the 1.8-litre cars only) was a hefty £1395.

In October 1997 the final changes were made to take the car into 1998 until the new model was introduced. Both the 1.8i and 1.6i received power steering as standard, and the 1.8iS wheels were changed to 6J x 15 five-spoke alloys - almost the same design as those found on the Harvard but with dished centres. At the same time, the 1.8i-based MX-5 Classic was launched. Finished in Brilliant Black, it featured black leather seat facings with red stitching, 15 inch five-spoke alloy wheels with locking wheelnuts, wood trim, a stainless steel rear brace bar, polished treadplates, a Momo leather steering wheel, floormats in black with red edging, 'Classic' badging and an RDS radio/cassette unit. It was priced at £17,495 on-the-road.

Sales throughout the British Isles continued to rise at an amazing rate. Mazda UK sold 4956 MX-5s during 1997, bringing the

Mazda MX-5

Dakar
Special Edition

The 1.8-litre MX-5 Dakar - only 400 were built for the British market. The advertising said: 'This car will become a timeless classic ...'

running total to an impressive 18,715 units.

The final version of the first generation MX-5 was announced in January 1998 - the Limited Edition Berkeley. Only 400 of these cars - finished in Sparkle Green Metallic - were produced. One of the main features was a black leather interior with contrasting light grey on the seat facings and door panels. Other niceties included 15 inch five-spoke alloy wheels with locking wheelnuts, a

The 1.6-litre Monza reached the UK market in May 1997. Finished in British Racing Green, this particular model was limited to 800 examples.

One of the last 1.8iS models to wear the now-familiar seven-spoke alloys. In October - for the 1998 Model Year in effect - the new five-spoke alloy wheels were adopted. The eagle-eyed will notice the fatter base on the door mirrors for cars with electrically-adjustable mirrors.

chrome boot rack, a stainless steel rear brace bar, stainless treadplates, dark burr wood trim, a Momo leather steering wheel, black leather gearlever and handbrake gaiter, a CD player and black floormats edged in grey. A numbered plaque was mounted on the centre console, and "Berkeley" badges were fitted just below the side indicators on the front wings. The Berkeley was priced at a very reasonable £17,600.

The home market

The range for the 1997 Model Year was unchanged from that which resulted from the reshuffle in the latter half of 1995; standard colour schemes were also unaltered. Prices had risen slightly over the last couple of years, but not by a great deal compared with those of the export markets. For instance, the basic model was 1,770,000 yen in Chiba (the author's Japanese home town situated near to Tokyo) in December 1996, while at the other end of the scale the V Special Type II started at 2,470,000 yen.

In August 1997 the SR Limited was announced to celebrate the eighth anniversary of the Eunos Roadster in Japan. Based on the M Package, the manual version (with Torsen limited-slip differential) weighed exactly 1000kg and was priced at 1,898,000 yen; the automatic weighed 30kg more and cost 1,978,000 yen.

Two colour options were available: Sparkle Green Metallic (the same colour as that for the British Berkeley) and Chaste White. Of the 700 examples produced white was the most popular shade, accounting for 384

Mazda UK's third special edition model of 1997 - the 1.8-litre Harvard.

sales. Features included highly-polished seven-spoke alloys, black leather seats with light grey nubuck-type inserts, chrome door mirrors, chrome dial surrounds, a CD/tuner and a Nardi leather gearknob. The standard Momo steering wheel with airbag was used (shortly after the SR Limited launch dual airbags became an option).

By this time more than enough cars had been sold on the home market to ascertain the various trends. The Special

Package was the most popular, accounting for roughly 40 per cent of sales. Japanese buyers buy mainly automatics, although only around 15 per cent of the Eunos Roadsters sold featured automatic transmission. The most popular colour, however, would not surprise anyone who has lived in Japan - it was white. Next in line was green, followed by black.

Japanese sales figures released for December 1997 confirmed the growing popularity of utility vehicles and MPVs in

The MX-5 Classic launched in the UK in October 1997.

Mazda MX-5 Berkeley

The 400-off Berkeley was announced in January 1998 and was the UK's final version of the first generation MX-5. Finished in Sparkle Green Metallic and with black and grey leather interior, it was priced at £17,600 and was basically very similar to Japan's SR Limited model.

Japan's SR Limited - the last special edition model for the home market. This example is shown in Sparkle Green Metallic but Chaste White was also available. In all, only 700 cars were built, with the white shade being the most popular colour.

preference to sportscars and coupés. The best-seller in the sporting line-up was the Toyota Corolla Levin with 722 sales for the month; the Celica managed 464 sales, while the Supra clocked up just 145 - the MR2 recorded a disappointing 91 sales. Mazda was also struggling with sales of 206 Eunos Roadsters and 202 RX-7s. The Nissan 300ZX and the rest of the Fairlady Z range found just 40 customers, although this was still quite a lot compared to sales of Honda's NSX supercar which amounted to only 13.

By comparison Honda sold 4230 of its CR-V and no fewer than 11,123 of its StepWagon people mover. In the smaller MPV class, Suzuki sold over 16,000 Wagon R models. Even executive cars were outselling sporting machines at a rate of almost ten to one! As the world's most dedicated followers of fashion, the Japanese were clearly telling manufacturers that the sportscar era was well and truly over unless they were offered something new. Eunos Roadster sales for the year totalled just 3537.

Fortunately, Mazda had its new car, but the MX-5 had started a roadster renaissance. It also left a lasting impression, making it into the final cut of 100 cars suggested for the "Car of the Century" title - one of only seven Japanese models (the Lexus LS400, Honda NSX and the first generation of Toyota Corolla, Honda Civic, Datsun Z and Mazda RX-7 made up the total) left in with a chance. Already a lot of superb cars have been dropped and the winner will be announced in December 1999. The

The family tree of the first generation Roadster for the home market.

second generation Eunos was eagerly awaited and, at the 1997 Tokyo Show, the car everyone wanted to see was finally unveiled ...

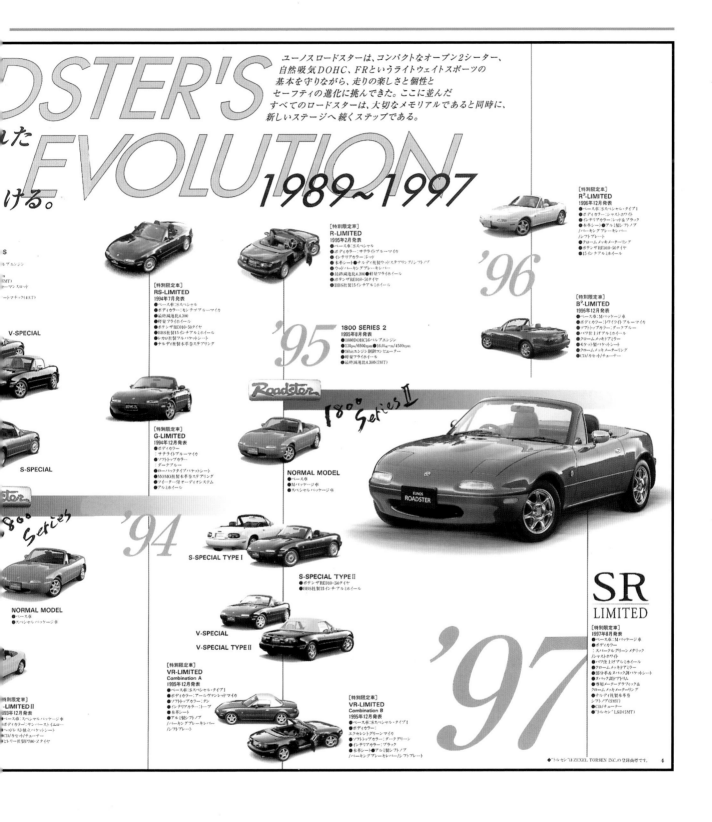

DSTER'S EVOLUTION 1989~1997

ユーノスロードスターは、コンパクトなオープン2シーター、
自然吸気DOHC、FRというライトウェイトスポーツの
基本を守りながら、走りの楽しさと個性と
セーフティの進化に挑んできた。ここに並んだ
すべてのロードスターは、大切なメモリアルであると同時に、
新しいステージへ続くステップである。

'96

'95

'94

'97

[特別限定車] R-LIMITED
1995年2月発表
●ベース車：Sスペシャル
●ボディカラー：サテライトブルーマイカ
●インテリアカラー：レッド
●本革シート＋ナルディ社製ウッドステアリング／シフトノブ
●ウッドパーキングブレーキレバー
●最終減速比4.300
●ボデンザRE010-50タイヤ
●BBS社製15インチアルミホイール

[特別限定車] RS-LIMITED
1994年7月発表
●ベース車：Sスペシャル
●ボディカラー：モンテブルーマイカ
●最終減速比4.300
●軽量フライホイール
●ボデンザRE010-50タイヤ
●BBS社製15インチアルミホイール
●レカロ社製フルバケットシート
●ナルディ社製本革巻ステアリング

1800 SERIES 2
1995年8月発表
●1800DOHC16バルブエンジン
●130ps／6500rpm 16.0kg・m／4500rpm
●16bitエンジン制御コンピューター
●軽量フライホイール
●最終減速比4.300（5MT）

[特別限定車] R²-LIMITED
1996年12月発表
●ベース車：Sスペシャル・タイプ1
●ボディカラー：シャスタホワイト
●インテリアカラー：レッド＆ブラック
●本革シート＋アルミ製シフトノブ
／パーキングブレーキレバー
／シフトプレート
●クローム・メッキドアミラー
●ボデンザRE010-50タイヤ
●15インチアルミホイール

[特別限定車] B²-LIMITED
1995年12月発表
●ベース車：Mパッケージ車
●ボディカラー：ツワイライトブルーメタリック
●ソフトトップカラー：ダークブルー
●バフ仕上げアルミホイール
●クローム・メッキドアミラー
●モケット製バケットシート
●クローム・メッキメーターリング
●CD／カセット付チューナー

[特別限定車] G-LIMITED
1994年12月発表
●ボディカラー
：サテライトブルーマイカ
●ソフトトップカラー
：ダークブルー
●ローバックタイプバケットシート
●MOMO社製本革巻ステアリング
●ツイーター付オーディオシステム
●アルミホイール

NORMAL MODEL
●ベース車
●Mパッケージ車
●スペシャルパッケージ車

S-SPECIAL TYPE I

S-SPECIAL TYPE II
●ボデンザRE010-50タイヤ
●BBS社製15インチアルミホイール

V-SPECIAL
V-SPECIAL TYPE II

V-SPECIAL

S-SPECIAL

NORMAL MODEL
●ベース車
●スペシャルパッケージ車

[特別限定車] VR-LIMITED Combination A
1995年12月発表
●ベース車：Sスペシャル・タイプ1
●ボディカラー：アールヴァンレッドマイカ
●ソフトトップカラー：タン
●インテリアカラー：ビーン
●本革シート
●アルミ製シフトノブ
／パーキングブレーキレバー
／シフトプレート

[特別限定車] VR-LIMITED Combination B
1995年12月発表
●ベース車：Sスペシャル・タイプ1
●ボディカラー：
エクセレントグリーンマイカ
●ソフトトップカラー：ダークグリーン
●インテリアカラー：ブラック
●本革シート＋アルミ製シフトノブ
●パーキングブレーキレバー／シフトプレート

[特別限定車] R-LIMITED II
●ベース車：スペシャルパッケージ車
●ボディカラー：サンバーストイエロー
●ヘッドレスト組込バケットシート
●CD／カセット付チューナー
●ピレリ社製P700-Zタイヤ

SR LIMITED
[特別限定車]
1997年8月発表
●ベース車：Mパッケージ車
●ボディカラー
：スパークルグリーンメタリック
／シャスタホワイト
●バフ仕上げアルミホイール
●クローム・メッキドアミラー
●部分革＋スパック調バケットシート
●スパック調ドアトリム
●専用メーターグラフィック＆
クローム・メッキメーターリング
●ナルディ社製本革巻
シフトノブ（5MT）
●CD／チューナー
●"トルセン" LSD（5MT）

◆"トルセン"はZEXEL TORSEN INC.の登録商標です。　4

This chapter concerns itself with the official MX-5-based specials like the show cars which have been exhibited through the years, the vehicles powered by alternative fuels and cars which came about because of the M2 project. Modified and tuned vehicles, including those by Mazdaspeed, are covered in the next chapter.

Club Racer

As well as the production models, Mazda decided to show a Miata-based car it called the 'Club Racer'

at the 1989 Chicago Show. MRA (*née* MANA) stylist Mark Jordan was credited with the sporty design.

The respected American journal *Road & Track* described the car in its May 1989 edition: 'In eyeball-splattering canary yellow, it featured fat Yokohama tires (205/50 ZR15 front, 255/45 ZR15 rear) faired into sweetly Coke-bottled sheet metal, a plastic rear cowl cover, six inch spoiler and teensy headlights under plastic covers. Shocks were Bilsteins,

The Club Racer was displayed alongside the production models at the Miata launch in Chicago. Apart from the obvious body changes, the Club Racer also featured a modified exhaust system.

body-coloured wheels were real/ fake Minilites by Panasport. Dee-lish.'

The interior was also modified to include leather trim, high-back seats (with the Miata logo and racing harnesses) and a Momo steering wheel. In effect, the aftermarket industry started the very day the car was launched!

M2-1001

The M2 project was established in November 1990 and the M2-1001 was the first offering. The four people involved were Mazda workers and included Hirotaka Tachibana (development engineer at the head of the M2 project) and Massanori Mizuochi, now Chairman of the Roadster Club of Japan. The main objective of the project was to be a direct contact between the company and the car's users, as well as building MX-5 specials for show purposes and test-marketing.

The M2-1001 was announced on 1 December 1991 (by which time the M2 team had settled down in its new headquarters in Setagaya, Tokyo), but deliveries didn't start until March 1992. The car featured a 130bhp engine linked to a five-speed manual transmission, a stiffened chassis, modified suspension and wider 195/50 R15 tyres mounted on eight-spoke alloy wheels. Finished in dark blue paint, the whole package weighed in at 960kg.

From the outset it was stated that only 300 examples were being built and this contributed greatly towards getting folk to part with a hefty 3,400,000 yen. For this kind of money, it was possible to buy a basic Nissan 300ZX, or a high-spec Toyota Supra in Japan. Nevertheless, the M2-1001 was heavily over-subscribed. In the end, a lottery system was used, resulting in many disappointed enthusiasts - Mazda could quite easily have sold at least 600 more!

M2-1002

After the phenomenal success of the M2-1001 one would be forgiven for believing that the 1002 couldn't fail. It was a similar scenario: 300 cars would be built - again finished in dark blue, but with a tan hood. The 1.6-litre engine was left as standard on this occasion (with a five-speed gearbox), as were the chassis details.

It was the interior that was the main feature on the 1002. Wood trim came from Yamaha and ivory leather was used almost everywhere. Even the top roll on the fascia was leather, but this time in dark blue. Without a doubt, the interior was truly beautiful and would have made any Italian coachbuilder proud. All this added an extra 10kg to the weight of its predecessor, despite it not having power steering (which 1001 had).

Announced at the end of 1992, deliveries of the 1002 started in February 1993. However, by the end of May when it was discontinued, only 100 of the 3,000,000 yen machines had been sold; some of the interior parts were later used on the Tokyo Limited of late-1993.

Failure of the 1002 was probably down to timing: remember, the MX-5 was launched at the height of an economic boom and people - especially in Japan - had plenty of money to spare for luxury items. The 1001 seemed to catch the mood of the moment; by the time the 1002 was launched, the economy had slowed down somewhat ... the bubble had burst. It is hard to imagine Japan struggling but, by all accounts, people were selling cars rather

The M2-1001 was the first product to be developed by the M2 project founded in November 1990. Announced in December 1991, the 1001 was obviously more muscular, but there were also a number of delightful touches such as the racing-style alloy fuel filler cap and door mirrors. Cars were numbered from 001 to 300.

Sadly, the M2-1002 was not as successful as the 1001. All M2 cars had unique tail badges and a numbered plate by the nearside door mirror. M2 numbers ran consecutively, so the 1002 series was allocated 301 to 400.

One of three electric MX-5s built to test the potential of alternative fuels. Mazda also built a hydrogen-powered MX-5 which proved the more practical of the two in everyday situations.

than buying them during this period and this goes a long way towards explaining the 1002's disappointing sales.

M2-1003 also concentrated on interior appointments (it also had a Rod Millen rear deck aero cover and BBS alloys), but after the 1002's disappointing response the project was shelved.

The MX-5 and alternative fuels

Development of the electric MX-5 had started in January 1992 and was scheduled to continue for two years. The project was set up with the objective of exploring alternative fuels, as environmental concerns were paramount in virtually every country around the world, not least in Japan which has had quite a strict policy since the 1970s.

In February 1993 Mazda UK released the following statement: 'Still very much a prototype project, as only three have been built, the battery-powered Mazda MX-5 was designed in conjunction with the Chugoku Electric Power Company and will be used by the company to run practicality tests of using electric cars on a daily basis.

'In testing, the electric Mazda MX-5 has achieved performance figures compatible with a petrol (gasoline)-driven 1.5-litre automatic. Powered by an electric AC motor, the energy source is taken from 16 nickel cadmium batteries situated in the engine bay. With a top speed of 80mph, acceleration of 0-25mph in just 4.2 seconds and a range of up to 111 miles, an electrically-powered MX-5 is being considered as a viable alternative for the future.'

Weight was the biggest problem. With power steering and air conditioning, the electric MX-5 weighed a hefty 1410kg in an unladen state, which was due to the 4 batteries up front and another 12 in the boot. In reality, only lighter and more compact batteries would ever make electric power a viable option in a car of this type.

Hydrogen power deserved

more careful consideration. Hydrogen does not emit hydrocarbons or carbon dioxide when it burns; it has high potential energy and can be used in all types of engines. In Japan the Ministry of International Trade & Industry (MITI) was intending to use hydrogen to gradually replace other energy sources. Mazda was called in to help with the project and conducted a year-long monitoring test in conjunction with the Nippon Steel Corporation's Hirohata works located near Kobe. R&D head Seiji Tanaka said: 'Our first objective is to use available fuels more efficiently by producing better engines. At present we are researching the Miller-cycle and developing lean-burn technology. Our second objective is to investigate alternative fuels such as natural gas and methanol and electric cars. But this will not cut pollution. Hydrogen offers many advantages over all these, especially electric cars, and with the rotary engine fuelled by hydrogen, performance is very close to the petrol engine.'

The hydrogen was stored in metal hydride powder, made up predominantly of titanium and iron. When the gas is cooled under pressure, the powder will absorb the atoms, allowing safe storage of a litre of gas in just one cubic centimetre of powder. Heating the powder releases the gas. The only problem with this method is that the boot is filled with aluminium canisters.

The hydrogen-powered car had a rotary engine from the normally-aspirated RX-7, but externally (apart from the obvious script down the sides of the vehicles), there was nothing to tell it apart from an MX-5 straight out of the showroom. It was the same story inside, the only exception being a more appropriate fuel gauge.

The electric car also looked surprisingly standard. Again, the fuel gauge was replaced, this time with a charge meter. The electric MX-5 was very quiet, but as I've said, not very quick. In fact, 0-62mph took 21.5 seconds - a figure that doesn't really stack up against 9.4 seconds for a petrol-driven machine. The hydrogen model, however, could reach the same yardstick speed in just 13.0 seconds, which is much more acceptable. It could also reach 93mph with a five-speed manual transmission. We shall have to wait and see whether or not hydrogen power has a future.

M2 finale

Despite the lack of a new model, the M2 team had been keeping itself busy since arrival of the M2-1002. In addition to 1003, many interesting projects had been carried out on various Mazda vehicles, but none was thought suitable for production for one reason or another. These projects included two particularly stunning Eunos Roadster-based machines that were, unfortunately, allowed to slip through the net - M2-1006 and M2-1008.

M2-1006 came about in mid-1992 and featured wider bodywork, RX-7 suspension and a 220bhp 3-litre V6 engine from the Sentia (929). Naturally, with this much power it was quite a handful, and to keep the car in check 225/50 VR16 tyres were fitted at the front with 245/50s at the back.

The M2-1008 was an attractive coupé, with a Club Racer type nose (complete with faired-in headlights) and a tail styled along the lines of the Ferrari Daytona - even the round rear lights seemed to pay tribute to the Pininfarina design, although single lamps were used on the Mazda instead of two on each side, as on the Italian car.

Before closing down the M2 operation in April 1995, the team did manage to get a third and final Eunos Roadster-based car into production - the M2-1028. Announced in February 1994 at a price of 2,800,000 yen, the car was based on the five-speed 1.8-litre model, but had a stronger yet lighter body (helped by a front strut brace and an aluminium roll-over bar) and a highly-tuned engine.

Tipping the scales at 960kg, it had 30 per cent better torsional rigidity giving improved resistance to bending; in fact, it was easily as strong as most closed cars. This, in addition to newly-developed Bridgestone tyres and a harder suspension set-up, allowed an impressive improvement in handling (0.93g has been measured on the skidpan). The 1028 was available in either a Dark Blue hue or Chaste White, although a hood was not supplied - at the end of the day, the car was intended to be more at home on the track than commuting to work on a daily basis!

Deliveries began in March

An M2-1028 finished in Chaste White. As well as a number of modifications to make the bodyshell stronger, the 1028 had a higher compression ratio, lightened flywheel, tuned ECU and a free-flow exhaust system. With 140bhp this was the most powerful M2 engine released to the public. M2-1028 numbers ran from 401 to 700.

The aggressive lines of the M-Speedster built on the so-called 'Mi-ari' - a car produced by the Irvine team to honour Ferrari at Monterey in 1994.

and of the 300 built, 185 were sold in white (the most popular car colour in Japan), leaving 115 finished in the blue shade. At least the M2 project went out on a high note as the M2-1028 sold out within a couple of months.

M-Speedster

The Miata M-Speedster made its debut at the 1995 Chicago Auto Show. It was designed by Wu-Huang Chin of MRA and featured a 200bhp, 1.8-litre supercharged engine. To keep the power in check, 215/50 ZR15 tyres were used, mounted on five-spoke alloy wheels. The braking system was also uprated with 250mm ventilated discs at the front and 225mm solid discs at the rear.

Complete Car was quite confident that this car gave an insight into the future, despite Tom Matano stating 'We have no intention of building it.' Perhaps the magazine thought it was being used as a tool to gauge reaction, as at the end of the article it wrote: 'If US buyers give the thumbs up, it will form the blueprint for a revamp in Europe.' Sadly, although there was almost universal praise for the machine, it was nothing more than a concept car.

M-Coupé

The M-Coupé was the third Miata-based concept car by MRA and it made its debut at the New York International Auto Show in April 1996. It resembled the M2-1008 above the waistline, but the M-Coupé was much nearer to standard below it.

There were differences, of course: twin round lights hid

The Miata M-Speedster made its debut at the 1995 Chicago Auto Show. Designed by Wu-Huang Chin of MRA, it featured a 200bhp, 1.8-litre supercharged engine.

under each pop-up cover (which looked very attractive), and there was a feature line running from the sill to just behind the door. The lines of the fibreglass roof panel merged beautifully with the rest of the body - the design was a credit to Tom Matano and his team.

This elegant coupé was powered by the stock B6-ZE

engine linked to a five-speed gearbox; 205/45 R16 Dunlop SP8000 tyres were employed, mounted on lightweight five-spoke alloy wheels. An interesting feature was the increased luggage space, created by moving the spare wheel to an underfloor position.

Again, Matano stressed that the M-Coupé was only ever meant

to be a styling exercise, but the favourable reaction it received from the public fuelled rumours that it might go into production. However, that was over two years ago and nothing has been heard since. With luck, there may be a closed version of the second generation MX-5.

The M-Coupé was first shown at the 1996 New York Show. The roof on this model was made from fibreglass but, had it gone into production, steel would have been used. Unlike the coupé developed by the M2 team, the rear lights on the MRA machine were standard Miata fare.

フロントバンパースポイラー ￥78,000
サイドステップ ￥60,000
リアアンダースポイラー ￥48,000
リアスポイラー ￥48,000
ハーフアップライトキット ￥88,000

シフトノブ ￥4,800
ステアリング ￥36,000

◆アルミホイール/アンドリューレーシングV F・R：7J-16＋30 ￥66,000
◆タイヤ/BS RE71Dラジアル F・R：205/45-16

ヨーロピアンタイプ
コンプリートメーター
￥99,000（ノーマル下取り価格）

ROADSTER
COMBAT MODEL

株式会社ヴェイルサイド
〒300-22 茨城県つくば市真瀬1250-3 TEL.0298-38-1104 FAX.0298-38-1106
＊記載事項は、平成7年5月現在のものです。 ＊表示価格には消費税は含まれておりません。 ＊撮影協力/岡田シティコア

VeilSide of Tsukuba offers a wide range of conversions on various popular Japanese sportscars. This is its stunning Roadster Combat Model.

MIATA MX-5 EUNOS

Only a few months after the MX-5 was announced, *Road & Track* was predicting a boom for custom parts. In the July 1989 edition it said: 'Mazda has set up the stock Miata for comfort more than handling. The ride is comfortably soft with more body roll than we would have expected. All of this is not to say that the Miata, with its light weight and short wheelbase, isn't quick and responsive; it's

The brochure from KG Works of Yokohama. The company's M-Coupé style twin headlight conversion (priced at 128,000 yen) is very elegant. Japan is full of companies like this offering body kits, cosmetic parts and tuning components, and to list them all would take a book in itself.

both. But it could be quicker and even more responsive. Already it is easy to see the aftermarket explosion this car is going to cause.' This observation was very astute; today, as well as a thriving custom scene, there's no shortage of companies around the world which supply enthusiasts with accessories. This chapter looks briefly at what can only be described as the MX-5 Industry.

Parts and accessories

In Japan, the choice of parts and accessories is immense. During 1994, Mazdaspeed, TRD (of Toyota fame) and Nismo (Nissan Motorsports International) joined forces to organise the Tokyo Auto Salon - an alternative motor show that caters purely for tuning and performance companies. In 1997 Mitsubishi Ralliart added its weight to the alliance and the four

companies became known collectively as "Works Tuning."

Apart from promoting the tuning business, Works Tuning also organises motorsport events in which owners can drive their cars at speed in controlled conditions. After all, if an owner fits high quality performance parts, it follows that he or she is going to want to try them out.

The author went to the 1997 Tokyo Auto Salon and was amazed at how big the event was. With around 900 cars on display, it attracted almost as many people as the Tokyo Show! The range of body kits, tuning parts and complete conversions was staggering. Some of the modifications are quite tasteful, others totally over-the-top.

As well as Mazdaspeed other higher-profile concerns were VeilSide, HKS, Racing Sports

Active, KG Works, Hayashi, Manatee, Garage Vary, Yours Sports, Dave Crockett and RE Amemiya Cars, but the list is practically endless. Indeed, *Hyper Rev* put together a book listing and describing the Eunos tuning scene in Japan - it amounted to over 200 pages!

Trust of Chiba developed a turbo kit, and a company called Cockpit even offered an MX-5 fitted with a 400bhp rotary engine. Knight Sports, better known for its excellent work on the RX-7, was also involved in supplying high performance parts for the Roadster.

The owners' clubs also got involved. One club, known as Barchetta, designed and marketed its own parts. A front fibreglass half-spoiler and bumper cover was available for 60,000 yen, while the attractive rear bumper was 100,000

yen. Smaller items were also listed, such as a gearshift gate box at just 6,000 yen.

HKS offered a full T-003 conversion; Pit Crew Racing's modifications made the Eunos look like an early TVR; Zoom designed a fairly convincing Lotus Elan lookalike, whilst others could offer nose panels shaped to resemble other vehicles like the Ferrari Daytona or the Nissan 300ZX. One concern even built a nose that reminded the author of a cross between the Daimler SP250 and Austin-Healey Sprite.

Of course, the full custom scene is much stronger in Japan where the cars are so much cheaper to buy (about the equivalent of £10,000 at the time of writing). In Britain, the purchase price and high residual value on the second-hand market puts most people off the idea of modifying their car too much, as it would affect the price when they came to sell it.

However, subtle modifications are commonplace. More restrained aftermarket components have become available almost overnight and the variety already rivals some of the established "classics" for range. For instance, the catalogue issued by Moss International Ltd (ironically, a company better-known for supplying parts for classic British marques such as MG and Triumph!) lists items like stainless steel exhaust systems and replacement catalytic converters, high-performance air filters, sparkplugs and leads, silicone hoses and a gel cell battery. Naturally, there are uprated suspension and braking components also, including strut tower and chassis braces.

For the interior there are leather seats - real or fake - wood trim kits, various gearknobs and steering wheels and leather gaiters for the gearlever and handbrake.

Kits are also available for interior lighting, electric windows, central and remote keyless locking and electronic boot release. There are also floor mats, stainless steel trim pieces for the sill tops, face vents and speakers and an aluminium pedal set. The catalogue also lists replacement soft tops, a hard top, wind deflector, boot spoiler, various luggage racks and boot trim components, including a hydraulic lift kit. Auxiliary lighting, a protective front grille, roll-over bar, car cover, Minilite-style alloys and a 7.5J x 16 wheel and tyre package make up the selection on offer.

Of course, the Moss catalogue is only one of many: Mazda lists the Finish Line range of accessories which includes detachable hard-top, alloy wheels, stereo upgrades, a rear spoiler, deck rack, polished treadplates and so on.

American magazines regularly feature the Miata Mania Accessories Catalog, 'jam-packed with products designed to improve and personalize your car.' Run down the classified ads and you'll find Motorsport of California, Racing Beat (which was involved in the success of the RX-7 in competition), Pacific Auto Accessories, Road Show International and goodness knows how many others. Performance Techniques and Cartech International have both produced a turbocharger installation; both Downing Atlanta and Nelson Superchargers of Los Angeles have gone down the supercharger route, and then there are the cars and accessories produced by Rod Millen and Mazdasports (see below). For

The Pit Crew Racing company of Suzuka offered this interesting conversion.

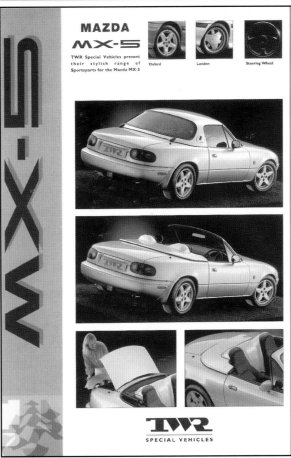

TWR of England produced this RTM hardtop, and a novel aero cover. The latter came in two parts: a moulding around the seats and a cover that butted up to it. This cover could then be removed and stored in the boot, allowing the softtop to be erected.

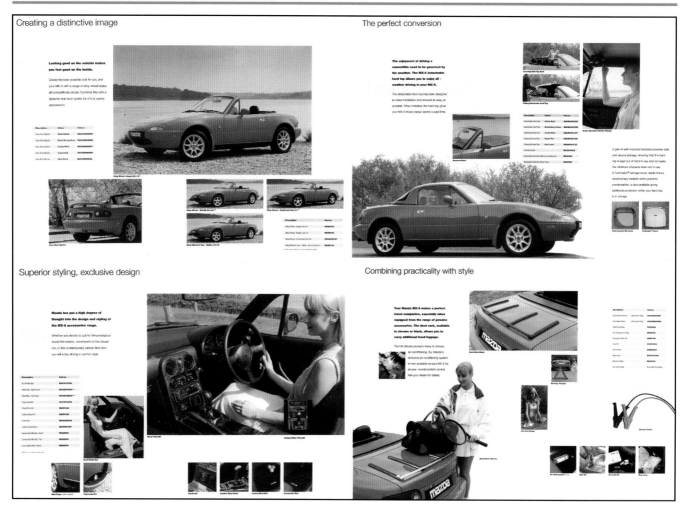

Pages from Mazda UK's official accessories catalogue of 1996.

something a little more adventurous, Performance Car Kraft of New Jersey offered Ford V8 conversion kits with uprated braking systems to suit.

In Germany, Samurai Tuning of Essen was quick to produce the Samurai MX5. With subtle modifications to the lower coachwork, a nice faired-in hood cover, rear spoiler and 225/50 ZR16 tyres on wide alloy wheels, it was quite a tasteful package.

Mazdaspeed

Mazdaspeed, the factory's racing subsidiary, lists shock absorbers with four different settings, harder springs that also lower the car by 30mm, thicker anti-roll bars, strut braces, plus harder shock mountings and lower arm bushes. It also stocks harder engine mountings, uprated brake pads for both front and rear and uprated clutch components. Special exhaust systems, pistons, camshafts, lightened flywheels, an oil cooler, a modified gearchange, high performance air filters and various viscous limited-slip differential units (plus a harder differential mounting rubber) round off the mechanical parts.

A number of engine tuning options are available, known as B-Spec modifications. Stage I takes a 1.6-litre engine to 130bhp, or a 1.8 to 145bhp. Stage II increases this to 144bhp on the 1.6, or 170 on the 1.8. There is also a supercharger kit which boosts the 1.6 engine's power to 170bhp and the 1.8-litre unit to 180bhp.

On the cosmetic side the list offers sportier-sounding exhaust tailpipes, replacement dashboards, steering wheels, alloy wheels, gearknobs (and with matching handbrake trim), various aerodynamic components and a bucket

Deliveries of Mazdaspeed's first complete car for the public - the C-Spec - started in April 1998. No more than 30 of these 200bhp machines would ever be produced, but at 4,350,000 to 5,300,000 yen, they were mightily expensive. The leather-trimmed model costs about the same as the Nissan Skyline GT-R V Spec.

seat. There's a roll-over bar which can also be specified with something Mazdaspeed call an "aeroboard" - a device to cut buffeting.

For some time, Mazdaspeed have listed the A-Spec Aero Kit Type I and Type II alongside the B-Spec engine tuning menu, but from April 1998 deliveries started on the most adventurous of the Tokyo-based company's projects - its first complete car for the public. Known as the Roadster C-Spec, and billed as "the final evolution," only 30 will ever be built. It features some rather stunning coachwork modifications, plus a 200bhp 2-litre Mazdaspeed Stage III engine. The basic version cost 4,350,000 yen, while the leather-trimmed Special was priced at 5,300,000 yen.

Modified packages in the USA

It is not surprising to learn that the Miata was soon the subject of a number of transformations in the States, some of which were done from a styling point of view, others from a performance angle. Occasionally, complete packages would be offered, a few of which are mentioned below.

Rod Millen, the New Zealander who has done so much to promote Japanese cars through his exploits in motorsport (he's represented Mazda, Toyota and Nissan at top level), was quick to see the potential in the Miata. Rod Millen Motorsport, operating from California, offered a turbocharged machine known as the Turbo MX-5 Miata.

As Richard Homan explained

in a 1989 *Road & Track* Special, 'On the engine side of things, the team was able to draw heavily from its experience with a similar 1.6-litre dohc 16v fuel-injected power-plant of Mazda origin - that of the turbocharged 323 GTX, a longtime bread-and-butter Millen rally car ... Millen Motorsport raided the 323 GTX's engine, pirating the car's camshafts, pistons (lowering the Miata's compression ratio from 9.4:1 to 7.2:1), and radiator, turbocharger and intercooler. The turbo implant is the golden nugget of the Millen Miata's performance upgrade. Tucked tightly into the engine bay, the little turbo is mounted stage left up against a Millen Motorsport-designed, stainless-steel exhaust manifold ...'

Power was put in the region of 230bhp but, despite this, the

Four pages from the Mazdaspeed brochure for the A-Spec Aero Kits. B-Spec modifications concentrate on the engine with various stages of tune being available.

standard gearbox was retained. A heavier clutch and a Millen limited-slip differential were used, however, as was an uprated suspension and braking package, the latter sourced from the RX-7 Turbo parts bin.

'Slung lower and filled out by the special 7J x 15 Rod Millen Motorsport directional aero wheels with 205/50 VR15 Bridgestone Potenza RE71R tyres, the Miata was beginning to look

tougher; it was getting an attitude ...' noted Homan.

Thus, every aspect of the Miata's performance was improved. 0-60 was covered in 6.4 seconds instead of the standard car's 9.5, and the standing-quarter was timed at 14.7 seconds (95.5mph terminal speed) - a full 2.3 seconds less. Top speed was 126mph.

As for handling, the moderate understeer usually found in the

stock Miata was reduced to mild understeer, helping the Millen car go through the slalom test quicker and pull 0.90g on the skidpan (against 0.83 for a standard model). Braking distances were reduced to 85 per cent of those recorded with a standard car.

Of course, everything comes at a price, and whereas the standard Miata cost $13,800, the fully-loaded Millen car was roughly $25,600. This included the

INTERIOR PARTS

⑨ステアリングホイール（φ360）
日本刀の「鍔」と同様、楕円形状のグリップ部断面をもつ本革巻き軽量ステアリングホイール。センター部分のベースはヘアライン加工したが、脱着式パッドも付けている。

⑩カーボンルックダッシュパネル
メーターパネルの表面をカーボン素材に調にプリントエ工し、コックピットにより話性とファッション性を高めたメーターセット（5アイテム）。ドライバーのスポーツ心を刺激するアイテム。フロントレンズ付。

⑪スポーツドライビングメーター
オフホワイトを基調に、レッドの文字色やエンジンの指針を効果的にデザインし、視認性とファッション性を高めたメーターセット（5アイテム）。

⑧スポーツシート

INTERIOR PARTS

ROLLBAR

STRUT BAR

ALUMINUM ALLOY WHEEL

⑰アルミホイール：MS-03

⑱アルミホイール：MS-01R

FUNCTIONAL PARTS

⑫ショックアブソーバー

⑬スポーツスプリングセット

⑭スタビライザー

⑮ラバーブッシュ

⑯クラッチカバー＆ディスク

⑰リミテッドスリップデフ

⑱ブレーキパッドセット

⑲ブレーキラインセット

⑳エキゾーストマニホールド

㉑スポーツサウンドマフラー タイプⅡ

㉒スポーツサウンドマフラー

㉓オイルクーラー

㉔エアフィルター

ROADSTER
TOURING KIT
A-SPEC.

---

turbocharger ($650), intercooler and plumbing ($2200), modified camshafts ($300), pistons ($120), fuel management system ($1100), stainless exhaust manifold ($550), stainless exhaust system ($330), Centreforce clutch ($425), uprated brakes ($2240), limited-slip differential ($750), larger anti-roll bars ($350), spring set ($200), strut brace ($225), Panasport 7J x 15 alloys ($740), exhaust temperature gauge ($350), boost gauge ($32), Momo steering wheel ($210), rear spoiler ($195) and rear deck aero cover ($195).

The package was sold in Australia under the Racing Dynamics name. Yokohama 195/50 ZR15 tyres were fitted on Venette 5-spoke alloys; otherwise it was very similar to the car in the States. Some thought the price a little high, but *Modern Motor* correctly pointed out that people happily paid a premium when the car was in short supply. The same Aussie magazine noted: 'Improving on a design so widely commended was a difficult task, but the modified car does the trick.'

Another company that transformed the standard Miata was Mazdasports of California - a newly-established arm of Oscar Jackson Racing (of Honda fame). Douglas Kott tried the car for *Road & Track* and was very impressed. He said: 'The well-scuffed

109

Rod Millen's Club Sport aero cover. Millen has also successfully marketed a whole string of complete conversions based around Japanese sportscars.

The Racing Beat body kit. So many bolt-on kits destroy the lines of the original, but one can still clearly see the distinctive MX-5 profile showing through on this restrained offering.

Japanese advertising for various American conversions.

Yokohama A008Rs adhered to the 200 foot-diameter skidpad with a vengeance to generate 0.89g - 7 per cent more grip than the stock Miata on the same surface. At the cornering limit, its balance was commendable; a drop-throttle stunt that would have had the driver of the stock car cranking in lots of countersteer required only a minor steering correction in the Mazdasports Miata to keep everything tidy and under control.'

Racing Beat built a number of

"California Miatas" to promote its aftermarket body panels. The full conversions included a new nose section, side skirts, a "Streamline" rear deck cover, rear spoiler and a restyled rear bumper.

Dave Hops of Monster Motorsports in California started modifying the Miata early in 1992. The "Monster Miata" conversion basically involves swapping the four-cylinder Mazda engine for a 225bhp 5-litre V8 from the Ford Mustang (complete with transmission), and then uprating suspension and braking components to suit. The brochure stated it was 'Where the Far East meets the Wild West!' Styling changes were amazingly subtle and resulted in the car looking like an M2 project, but performance freaks are usually more interested in figures - 0-60 in under five seconds. More than 70 examples had been built within the first four years, but in the meantime, Hops introduced the "Mega Monster."

The Mega Monster, styled by

Terry Choy, could be bought with a supercharged 5-litre unit giving 400bhp, or a 5.6-litre producing an incredible 460bhp! Strangely, because the Mazda 1.8-litre four-cylinder engine is not particularly light, the Mega Monster conversion added only 120kg to the weight of the car. Thus, even the 400bhp machine is capable of 0-60mph in less than four seconds and will happily go on to the claimed maximum of 160mph. The number of Mega Monsters built is not as great as that for Monster Miatas. Those not put off by its brute power might flinch at the $50,000 price tag. Hops was also working on the Miata FXR - a turbo conversion boosting the 1.8-litre engine output to a more reasonable 195bhp.

Another professional conversion was carried out by Dave Lemon of Mazdatrix, another California company more usually associated with the rotary engine. Not surprisingly, Lemon - an ex-racing driver - used an RX-7 Turbo power-unit to improve the performance of the Miata. With around 260bhp on tap, 0-60 came up in just 6.6 seconds, so suspension and braking were suitably uprated to keep the car in check. The detailing was beautiful ...

In early 1995 Car & Driver carried an article on the PFS Miata SC. PFS stood for Peter Farrell Supercars, a Virginia-based company run by Farrell, an ex-racer who became heavily involved with Mazda's competition success in the States. Apart from selling the occasional 360bhp RX-7, Farrell also commissioned Craig Neff (who built pop group ZZ

Top's famous Cad-zilla) to build the supercharged Miata SC. With 185bhp on tap, the 0-60 time came down to 6.9 seconds, whilst top speed was now around 130mph. Naturally, the suspension was uprated and the Miata SC actually pulled a full 1.0g on a 300 foot skidpan. Production models were priced at $30,000.

Buying hints and tips

There is no doubt that the MX-5 has caught the imagination of the motoring public. In March 1996 Auto Express said: 'This roadster is guaranteed to put a smile on your face. It looks great and provides the sort of driving pleasure few cars can match.' Popularity like this means plenty of opportunity for making money and, whilst the majority of people dealing in the MX-5 and its aftermarket add-ons are as straight as the day is long, Auto Express highlighted a new problem that every potential buyer should be aware of - secondhand cars which are imported from Japan that have either been damaged or are no longer able to pass the strict tests carried out in that country after a car reaches its third birthday.

In mid-1997 Auto Express found that a large number of cars were coming into Britain with service histories in Japanese and/or which had been involved in accidents. The engine management systems are different and all Japanese market vehicles are fitted with kph speedometers, giving an ideal opportunity to alter the mileage once it is replaced with an mph speedo. It has also been stated that Japanese market cars

do not have the same rust protection as do British market cars. The author took a British car out to Japan and - believe me - there is much more to it than simply changing the registration number ...

The MX-5 will hold its value well, regardless of whether or not it's a limited edition model. In fact, Mazda UK issued a press release which referred to an in-depth study to find the lowest depreciating cars in the UK carried out by What Car? magazine. The MX-5 was placed in the under £17,500 price category and the release read as follows: 'The What Car? survey in the July 1991 issue was conducted in order to advise its readers of which new cars would suffer from the smallest amount of depreciation within the first 12 months of ownership. A total of 20 vehicles were assessed, with the Mazda marque taking three places.

'The Mazda MX-5, currently What Car? magazine's Sports Car of the Year, was judged overall winner with the judges commenting: "It's appealing on the road for all the right reasons - steering accuracy, delightful gearchange quality, great handling ability and carefree wind-in-the-hair motoring." The What Car? panel determined that the Mazda MX-5 would depreciate by only 15 per cent in the first 12 months.' Next in line was Toyota's MR2 (17 per cent), followed by the BMW 318i at 20 per cent. The Mazda still commands a high resale value today (it received the What Car? award again in 1997).

The moral of the story is there's rarely a true bargain: if an

MX-5 is cheap, be careful. Ask plenty of questions, insist on seeing its service history and have the car inspected by a professional body. If the car's been modified, make sure it has been done properly.

Running an MX-5

The best advice one can offer here is join an owners' club. Unlike most car clubs which only come into being once a model attains "classic" status (usually based on age, examples getting scarcer and parts more difficult to source), the MX-5 had organisations popping up all over the world the minute it was launched.

In America, Norman Garrett (who, as you will have learnt from reading the earlier sections of the book, was heavily involved with the car while he was with MANA), founded the Miata Club of America. By the end of 1989 it was estimated to have almost 5000 members, and today that figure hovers around the 25,000 mark. With Chapters (branches) all over the country, combined membership experience means that someone, somewhere will have had a similar problem and, more importantly, found a way of overcoming it. There is even a UK Chapter (the MX-5 Owners' Club), with Hamish McLean currently holding the post of Chairman. Paul Grogan, ex-Chairman and co-founder of the club, kindly helped with some of the information for this book.

In Japan, as one would expect, there are numerous clubs. The biggest was founded by ex-M2 project man, Massanori Mizuochi,

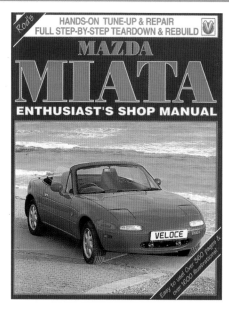

The Mazda Miata/MX-5 Enthusiast's Shop Manual - a great investment for MX-5 owners.

who is now Chairman of the Roadster Club of Japan. This club came about in 1996 when a large number of smaller organisations decided to group together.

Rod Grainger of Veloce Publishing produced the *Mazda MX-5 Enthusiast's Workshop Manual* (known in America as the *Miata Enthusiast's Shop Manual*) to help owners complete DIY jobs on their car. It is probably the most useful £20 an MX-5 owner could ever spend; there's helpful advice on every aspect of MX-5 ownership. The manual currently covers all 1.6-litre models up to 1994 but will soon be expanded to include newer vehicles. A manual which covers the 1.8-litre car is also in preparation for publication early in 1999.

The MX-5 is not a complicated car to work on, which is a good thing as the engine oil and air cleaner should be changed on a

very regular basis if the car is to be kept in optimum condition. It is also recommended that the gearbox oil is renewed more often than the service schedules specify.

It's worth remembering that - with the exception of basic service items - MX-5 parts are quite (and sometimes very) expensive, but mechanical components have so far proven very reliable if the car is properly maintained. Refer to Rod's manual for the best possible advice, but other than the kind of wear and tear one would expect as mileage increases, there isn't really that much to look out for. Apart from badly repaired crash damage, there shouldn't be much of a problem with the body either, but it's worth checking under the wheelarches just in case. One important point: the hood's rear screen is very susceptible to scratching and damage and is not easy to replace.

Seeing as we started this chapter with modifications, please note that the type of work involved in tuning and upgrading cars more often that not requires someone qualified to do the work. Even something as simple as putting wider wheels and tyres on the car may interfere with the geometry (and sometimes the body) unless the rolling diameter and offset are the same. Before attempting anything, it may be worth asking if someone in your local club has tried a similar operation, or if the club can recommend a specialist. Also, always remember to inform your insurance company of any changes, however minor they may seem to you.

7
The Second Generation

A drawing from the Hiroshima studio. The back looked like a Jaguar XK8.

Mazda had obviously found a winning formula with the MX-5/ Miata/Eunos - sales of well in excess of 400,000 units in such a short space of time is testimony to that fact - but it was inevitable that sooner or later the popular sports-car was going to need a facelift.

Although sales were still strong in parts of Europe (the UK especially), they were gently falling off in America and quite rapidly in Japan. The first generation (or M1) model could have carried on at these levels, but it was obvious that the older car wouldn't pass the stricter crash regulations planned for 1999.

Mazda therefore called upon its Technical Research Centres in Japan (Hiroshima and the Yokohama branch completed in mid-1987), America (the MRA team in California) and Germany (the European R&D centre, known by the initials MRE, was completed in May 1990 and situated in Oberusel on the outskirts of Frankfurt), to put forward their ideas. The brief was to update the car and make it meet forthcoming

regulations, but to keep its character intact.

Speaking in 1990, John Ebenezer, Mazda UK's Chairman, said: 'Few people are aware of Mazda's total commitment to producing more than just pedestrian cars and the Technical Research Centres are essential weapons in achieving this ambition. What makes them so unique and particularly exciting is that the Japanese have insisted upon a high level of local ideas and input. The result is that while most of the personnel in the Hiroshima and Yokohama centres are obviously Japanese, over 80% of the Irvine and Frankfurt centres staff are American and European respectively. What is particularly pleasing for me as a Briton is the fact that four of the department heads in Frankfurt are British, and have all, incidentally, been recruited from Porsche ...'

Mazda is quite unusual for a Japanese company in that of the top 35 positions at the end of 1997, eight were held by foreigners, due mainly to Ford's involvement. One

MIATA MX-5 EUNOS

Another Hiroshima design sketch, this time with covered headlights. However, the consensus of opinion was to go with the exposed lights, and a number of clays were duly made incorporating this feature.

of them, Henry Wallace, joined the Mazda Board in 1993 along with two other Ford executives, and became President three years later. He was thus the first *gaijin* [foreigner] to hold the presidency of a Japanese car company.

It is interesting to note that Ford (which had increased its share in the Japanese company to 33.4 per cent on 12 April 1996, thereby achieving a controlling interest), left the Mazda team alone to develop the car, asking only that the project be 'speeded along.' It's also interesting that although sportscar sales were in a downward spiral compared to sales of RVs and MPVs, Ford still backed the M2 Roadster project, despite 1997 being a bad year financially (share values dropped almost 8 per cent). It was actually a far braver decision than it had been for the first generation; the market was smaller and there were more competitors. However, compared to the situation in Korea, the Japanese company had little to worry about.

A fresh face

Unlike the competition held as part of the OGG project (which ultimately led to the first generation MX-5), there were no winners or losers with the second generation. Mazda simply wanted ideas from its various design centres and the whole project was overseen by Martin Leach.

The Hiroshima proposal in various stages of development

One of the design sketches submitted by the Yokohama office. This design was intended to keep the pop-up headlamp style of lighting.

The Frankfurt office submitted some stunning designs, but they were not destined to be developed further.

Two views of the clay made to represent the Yokohama design. The author feels that this was an exceptionally pretty car, but the design was rejected.

With shades of the original remaining, Irvine's design was nonetheless far more muscular.

A front view of Irvine's design - already strong second generation (M2) features were showing through.

One of the clays built using the Ken Saward drawings as a basis. This was the design that would be developed into the second generation model.

Takao Kijima - Chief Engineer for the second generation MX-5.

Koichi Hayashi - Mazda's Chief Designer for the second generation MX-5.

Each centre was given the same brief: keep the car's character intact. Tom Matano gave an interesting example of how the new car should be designed: 'Looking from 100 metres away, a person should recognise the vehicle is a Miata. From 50 metres, it will still appear to be a Miata, but as it gets closer still, they will realize it is the new model.'

The amazing thing is that all of the designs were very similar, but as everyone started from the same point it's perhaps not so surprising. From sketches, each centre (except the Frankfurt studio) produced full-sized clays which were presented for inspection at a meeting in Hiroshima.

Quite soon, the Yokohama office proposal fell by the wayside, leaving the Irvine and Hiroshima offerings from which the choice would be made. After much deliberation, the MRA design (credited to Ken Saward - an ex-Chrysler man) was the one chosen for development.

Evolution, not revolution

Tentative development work towards the 'full model change' had started in the spring of 1994, but it wasn't until November 1995 that the project began in earnest, by which time the first batch of mechanical mules was already undergoing extensive testing. Takao Kijima had been appointed Chief Engineer of the MX-5 in July 1995, meaning responsibility for the second generation fell on his shoulders. Incidentally, his predecessor, Yoshioka, became Chief Chassis Engineer in the Development Centre.

Kijima, who had been with Mazda since 1967, was an important member of the team which had developed the first MX-5, and was also highly-respected for his work through the years on the RX-7. Koichi Hayashi, who had worked on the first generation body alongside Matano, was Chief Designer.

In May 1997, the excellent Japanese magazine *Car Graphic* published an interview with Takao Kijima. A lot of clues were given about the new MX-5; for instance, it would definitely continue to have a front engine, rear drive layout, and the wheelbase and suspension set-up would stay much the same. Dual airbags and stricter safety and emissions regulations were obviously going to add weight. In fact, at one point it was thought that up to 60kg would be added. However, a light package was crucial; according to Kijima it was apparently 'hard work to find the balance between strength and weight, but to make an all-aluminium chassis like the [Lotus] Elise would make the car too expensive.'

Kijima also wrote an essay outlining the aims of the design team. It read as follows: 'In the eight years since the Rebirth of the Lightweight Sports Roadster in the form of the Mazda MX-5, more than 430,000 agile and friendly roadsters have been delivered to the world's enthusiasts, rekindling a powerful flame among them for exhilarating open-air motoring and imparting the joy of "Oneness between the Car and Driver."

'We at Mazda are firm believers in continuous improvement. A sportscar must be thoroughly contemporary and up to date, incorporating the latest technological developments. To rest on your laurels is to stagnate and fall behind. The original MX-5 has thus been constantly refined, including two major updatings and numerous improvements, to answer our customers' expectations and requirements.

'The last decade of the century has seen giant leaps in technology, particularly in electronics, but also in design, development and manufacturing of the automobile. At the same time, society's concern about safety and environmental issues has become more acute. We decided that the MX-5 must progress to meet the challenges of the 21st century. We will accomplish this by further enhancing the lightweight open sportscar's dynamics and meeting all social requirements.

'There was one fundamental principle guiding Mazda's design and engineering team for the new MX-5's personality: "We must value and assert the MX-5's inborn Soul, and train, strengthen and refine the Body." The new car required no conceptual revision. Enhance the virtue of the compact, lightweight, two-seat open sportscar, and offer a sportscar unparalleled in ownership delight and driving pleasure, to people of all walks of life, young and young at heart. We pursued new dimensions in open-air motoring, fun-to-drive and styling.

'With the objectives clearly established, we pursued three key areas of development:

1) Joy of open-air motoring, in comfort and ease: The new MX-5 is to be enjoyed primarily as an open sportscar at all speeds and even in winter, barring extremely inclement weather. We were able to accomplish this goal with innovative design and features.

2) True sportscar driving fun: "Oneness of the Car and Driver" enables the driver to fully exploit the new MX-5's exciting, natural and safe performance potential. The development team's aim of instinctive "drive-by-wish" precision was realised. Sounds are important ingredients in sportscar driving. Thus, the new MX-5's engine and exhaust are tuned to delight the ears of the driver, passenger and onlookers.

3) Thoroughly modern yet unmistakable MX-5 styling: the instantly recognisable exterior design carries the lineage of the original MX-5 in a balanced, masculine manner, and the interior stimulates enthusiasm the instant you climb behind the wheel.

'The car's everyday practicality has also been improved, including a larger and more usable luggage compartment. Safety has been greatly enhanced by incorporating a highly rigid body structure and a standard dual SRS airbag system for all models.

'With this new model, we believe that we have extended the enjoyment of the fun of the lightweight sportscar to a much larger audience.

'We fully utilized the latest

Mazda Digital Innovation system (MDI), to incorporate numerous technological advancements into the design, to aid development, and to further improve build quality. The creation of an automobile is ultimately the work of people. And our team dedicated all its effort to ensuring that the sporting Soul of the original MX-5 now dwells within the safe and strong new Body.'

Kijima felt it was important to further improve the car's best points and not allow the areas in which it was weak to lose ground against the competition. He had actually consulted Hirai on a number of aspects concerning the project, and also tested all those vehicles from competitors that had come onto the market since the Eunos Roadster's introduction, noting their strengths and weaknesses. In essence, he wanted to enhance the Mazda's performance, handling, sound and driving sensations,whilst at the same time keeping the car affordable.

Engine

Kijima's interview in *Car Graphic* promised a 1.8-litre engine with a lightened flywheel (the 1.8-litre gave a better match for cars with automatic transmission), whilst a 1.6-litre unit available in Europe would attract lower insurance. The exhaust note had again been tuned (noise limits caused a few problems here), and there was also a hint of a six-speed manual gearbox.

With a number of revisions it was hoped that the existing 1839cc BP-ZE (RS) unit would produce 145ps at 6500rpm, while the 1597cc

Awesome performance - just as it should be

Gaze upon the fabulous body of the new Mazda MX-5 and it's obvious that here is a car that was born to perform. Turn on the ignition and the resonant sound that greets you then confirms its performance potential in true roadster fashion.

How this performance manifests itself depends on which of the two new engines is selected: either the fast yet frugal 1.6 litre, 110 bhp unit or the higher power 1.8 litre, 140 bhp powerplant. With four valves per cylinder and fuel injection, both deliver masses of low-down torque for instant pick-up from low revs and produce just the sort of spirited response that's expected of a thoroughbred sports car. And, of course, standard in every engine is Mazda's legendary reliability.

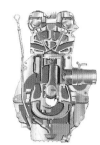

The new engines deliver superb performance and exceptional economy.

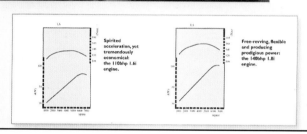

Spirited acceleration, yet tremendously economical: the 110bhp 1.6i engine.

Free-revving, flexible and producing prodigious power: the 140bhp 1.8i engine.

The engine specifications, as seen in the UK catalogue. (Yes, they've got the engine cutaway back to front.)

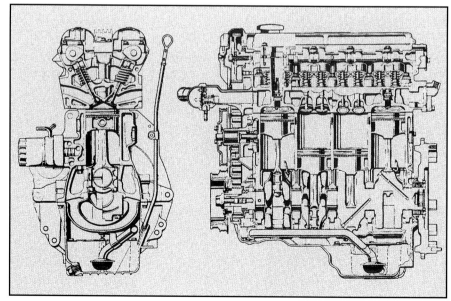

Cutaway drawings of the 1.8 litre BP-ZE (RS) power-unit.

B6-ZE (RS) engine was given a target of 125ps at the same revs. This represented about 10 per cent more power than before, assuming one takes the original 1.6-litre specification as the starting point.

After the intake and exhaust system was refined (the Variable Intake Control System - or VICS - was employed) under the direction of Yoshiaki Daikara, and different pistons (to give a higher compression ratio), camshaft profiles and a remapped ECU were adopted, the Japanese catalogue confirmed that these targets had been met. European specifications, however, suggested a shortfall of 5ps on the 1.8 and no less than 15ps on the smaller engine. In the American market the 1.8-litre four-cylinder unit's output was quoted at 140bhp at 6500rpm, with 119lb/ft of torque at 5500rpm.

Drivetrain

Kijima's hint at a six-speed gearbox became reality, but - sadly - only for the 1.8-litre cars for the home market (there has been talk of the possibility of a six-speed for the year 2000 in the US, perhaps even with an uprated engine, but this is certainly not a foregone conclusion). As the press release noted: 'The type BP 1.8-litre engine is equipped with a new six-speed

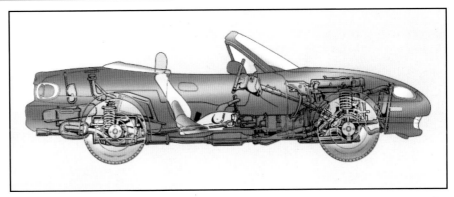

A cutaway drawing showing the layout of the second generation model.

manual transmission. The sixth gear performs as an overdrive, contributing to sportier driving with optimum performance including revving and acceleration at higher speeds.

'Both six-speed and five-speed manual transmissions use the short-stroke type stick-shift and promise quick shifting with a flick of the wrist. The transmission achieves higher rigidity from the improved internal synchronized system, producing quick yet precise handling even during severe shifting.'

The six-speed gearbox (type Y16M-D, jointly developed with the Aisin concern) brought the gears closer, of course, which would silence the critics who thought the difference in revs from second to third - and third to fourth, in particular - was too great

on the original car, considering how high up the rev range peak torque came in. The five-speed manual gearbox was of the M15M-D type, incidentally. Gear ratios and final drives were different for various markets (see table).

Naturally, the four-speed automatic gearbox (type SB4A-EL) had different ratios again, but it should be noted that in Japan the 1.6-litre cars had a 4.3:1 final drive, while the 1.8s had a 4.1:1 unit. The 4.1:1 ratio was also used in America, but the automatic option was not listed for Europe. A semi-automatic transmission was apparently not even considered; although quite fashionable, it was deemed not pure enough for a back-to-basics sportscar.

A Torsen limited slip differential came on the manual 1.6-litre Special Package and manual 1.8-litre cars in Japan, and as part of the Popular Equipment Package in the States. In Europe, it came on the higher-grade 1.8-litre machines as standard. The PPF transmission brace was carried over from the first generation.

Chassis

Koji Tsuji was put in charge of the

	Japan 1.6	Japan 1.8	USA 1.8	Europe 1.6	Europe 1.8
1st	3.136	3.760	3.136	3.136	3.136
2nd	1.888	2.269	1.888	1.888	1.888
3rd	1.330	1.645	1.330	1.330	1.330
4th	1.000	1.257	1.000	1.000	1.000
5th	0.814	1.000	0.814	0.814	0.814
6th	-	0.843	-	-	-
f/d	4.3:1	3.91:1	4.3:1	4.1:1	4.1:1

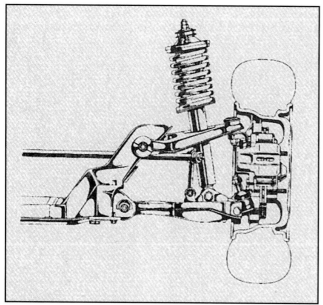

The front suspension.

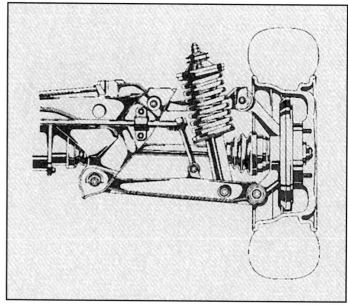

The rear suspension.

chassis, and to quote from the Tokyo Show press release: 'The front-engine rear-drive layout is maintained, achieving an ideal front and rear weight distribution and optimum enjoyment of control. The engine is mounted midship behind the front axle. The battery and temporary tyre are placed under the trunk floor. This provides a lower centre of gravity and increased trunk space. Lowering the front overhang weight and placing all the heaviness as close to the vehicle centre as possible allowed us to achieve superb yaw inertia moment and ideal 50:50 weight distribution.

'The new Roadster adopts a further refined double wishbone suspension, which was well-known on the first generation. The carefully tuned suspension geometry was completely reviewed to optimize driving pleasure ... while adding to the vehicle's driving stability. The new damper and coil spring units are individually off-set mounted to minimize transmission of road noise to the body.

'The four-wheel disc brake system is ventilated in front and solid at the rear. The brake system provides precise braking performance.

'The vehicle has rack-and-pinion steering. With the lock-to-lock 2.6 turns, it creates a direct yet quick handling feel. The overlapping effects of the re-adjusted suspension settings and reduced yaw inertia moment achieve extraordinary manoeuvrability.'

One or two points need further explanation - the new suspension settings made the car understeer less and much easier to drift through corners. As for the brakes, ABS was available but rarely standard (see the next chapter). Power steering came on most cars and again the next chapter outlines the various specifications - American models were listed at 3.2 turns lock-to-lock, or 2.7 with the speed-sensitive power-assisted steering.

Wheel designs were revised yet again with pressed steel or light alloy options available. The five-spoke alloy wheels came in 14 or 15 inch versions but looked very similar. The details of those supplied to the various markets are covered in the following chapter.

Body

Hayashi was basically given a free hand, but he said: 'I wanted to let the feeling of the old model live on, because I thought it didn't need changing to any great extent. The original, in the mould of a 1960s British lightweight sportscar, was perfect. However, the new body is more three-dimensional and muscular, with some exciting elements. The rich shapes can be viewed from any angle.'

The new body incorporated the Mazda Advanced Impact Distribution and Absorption System, which helped increase

A word from Koichi Hayashi (Chief Designer on the M2 body)

Miho Long: 'What was the hardest part of the design?'

Mr Hayashi: 'Actually, the toughest part was the very first step - deciding on which direction the design should take. 'We had to make a decision on how to improve a car that was already accepted worldwide, and therefore had to bear in mind how the design of the second generation would fit into the Roadster's history. We also had to consider what sort of design theme was the most suitable expression for a contemporary Mazda sportscar. 'I struggled to come to a conclusion regarding how to improve the car, so as a result I decided not to change the image of the first generation too much, keeping the original concept, but at the same time giving the vehicle a more sporty and modern feel.'

Miho Long: 'Could you tell us what is your favourite part of the body, and why?'

Mr Hayashi: 'Definitely the rear fender [wing]. I wanted to give it a dynamic feel, an accent for the whole body. This part of the body surface has a real feeling of tension, yet still has a comfortable atmosphere from any angle - it was finished exactly the way I wanted it. Personally, I love the view one gets of this area from the rearview mirror when I'm driving!'

Body prototypes in various stages of development. The basic styling was obviously decided very early in the proceedings, as only detail changes were made on each of these four models (see also following pages).

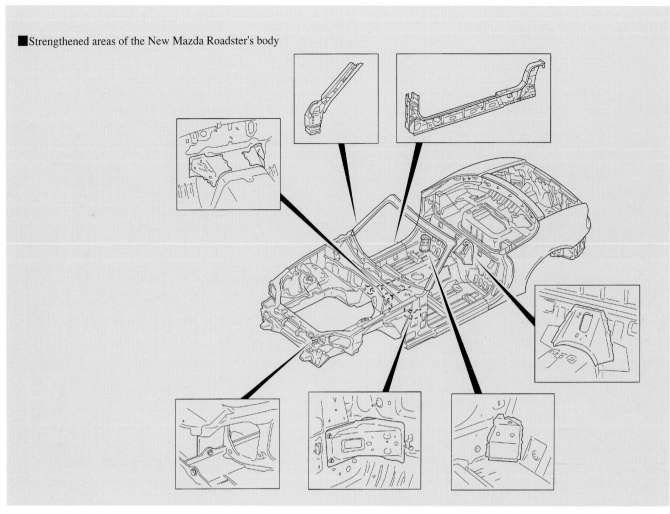

■Strengthened areas of the New Mazda Roadster's body

The body was designed with the help of computers. Mazda's Digital Innovation helped strengthen the body in key areas (mainly at each end of the transmission tunnel, in the sills, and at the base of the A-pillars), whilst at the same time keeping the weight down to a minimum.

passenger safety in the event of an accident. The front and rear crumple zones effectively absorbed impact energy from both directions. Beefier sills (rockers) minimized body distortion in the case of side impact, aided by twin bars inside the door panels.

At the same time this enhanced body rigidity provided an excellent basis for the suspension; reinforcement of the suspension's mounting points naturally had a direct effect on handling.

After almost 30,000 stress measurements were taken on the all-steel unitary body, it was estimated that overall rigidity had increased by 38 per cent.

In all, only around 40 per cent of the new body was carried over from the M1 model. Virtually all of the panels were new, including the floorpan, but due to the limited budget the windscreen, windscreen surround and most of the cowl were carried over - this at least meant that the original

hardtop could still be used with the second generation car.

The wings were more muscular in shape (adding a little to the overall width of the vehicle, even though it went against Kijima's express wish 'not to add a single millimetre'), with the lines flowing over into the bonnet, while the doors now had a large radius curve at the bottom of the trailing edge (a feature found on the RX-7), and Tanaka's original door handles were dropped in

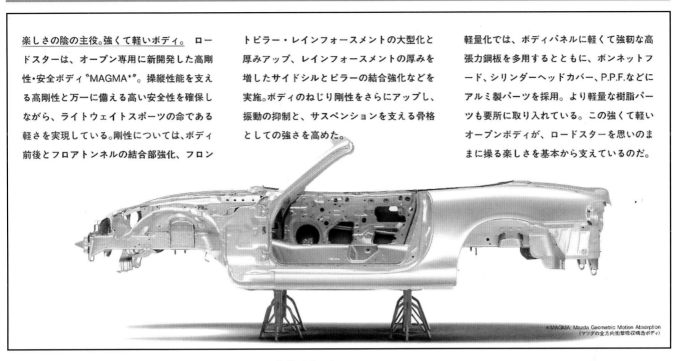

楽しさの陰の主役。強くて軽いボディ。 ロードスターは、オープン専用に新開発した高剛性・安全ボディ〝MAGMA*〟。操縦性能を支える高剛性と万一に備える高い安全性を確保しながら、ライトウェイトスポーツの命である軽さを実現している。剛性については、ボディ前後とフロアトンネルの結合部強化、フロン

トピラー・レインフォースメントの大型化と厚みアップ、レインフォースメントの厚みを増したサイドシルとピラーの結合強化などを実施。ボディのねじり剛性をさらにアップし、振動の抑制と、サスペンションを支える骨格としての強さを高めた。

軽量化では、ボディパネルに軽くて強靭な高張力鋼板を多用するとともに、ボンネットフード、シリンダーヘッドカバー、P.P.F.などにアルミ製パーツを採用。より軽量な樹脂パーツも要所に取り入れている。この強くて軽いオープンボディが、ロードスターを思いのままに操る楽しさを基本から支えているのだ。

*MAGMA: Mazda Geometric Motion Absorption
（マツダの全方向衝撃吸収構造ボディ）

A finished monocoque.

favour of more modern items in body colour.

The sill panels look heavier (as Tom Matano put it, they have 'more drama'), merging with the leading edge of the door to give a distinctive styling feature. The centre line has been deleted between the wheels, but where the bumpers join the body there are still remnants of the M1's centre line.

The familiar pop-up headlights were deleted in favour of fixed ellipsoid lenses in a bid to save weight at the front, while manual operation of the hood was kept to avoid the weight of electric motors and complicated mechanism that a power-operated hood would require. Losing the pop-up headlights shed 5.6kg from the overall weight of the vehicle and also improved the car's aerodynamics (there was quite a dramatic difference in Cd readings).

Moving back, the centre edge of the bootlid incorporated a duck-tail lip to improve aerodynamics (as well as the high-level rear brake light, the new Mazda badge and numberplate lights), while up front an aluminium bonnet was employed once again, despite the need to save money. The air intake is larger than before and both bumpers look less dainty - the lines found in the sills continue through to the lower edge of the bumpers.

Interestingly, the rear panel that carries the numberplate and badging is now part of the bumper assembly instead of separate. (Or more correctly, two separate pieces from a manufacturing point of view as the first generation home market had its own panel that fitted neatly around the number-plate.) Now all markets had the same specification.

As well as the front lights, the rear lights were also modified but not quite as drastically. The main point of the exercise was to incorporate the rear fog light into the design (for the markets that required one), thus removing the need for a separate item mounted under the bumper. Door mirrors were now sharper-looking affairs - longer and narrower.

Overall dimensions of the new Roadster were as follows: length: 3955mm; width: 1680mm; height: 1235mm; wheelbase: 2265mm. Ground clearance was 135mm, and front and rear track were 1405 and 1430mm respectively, representing a 10mm increase in the rear track. The body was therefore slightly shorter but 5mm wider; height and wheelbase were unchanged. With the hood up, the Cd was recorded at 0.36

(the original was 0.38).

The possibility of a coupé was raised during the *Car Graphic* interview with Kijima, to which the disappointing reply was 'I don't think so.' The opinion was that it was somewhat pointless trying to make the car as light as possible if there was going to be a coupé too. This is a shame as many people admired the M-Coupé; when it was introduced in 1996 Mazda said that if reaction was favourable - which it was - it might go into production. In reality, it is probably truer to say that Mazda didn't want the possibility that an MX-5 coupé might steal some of the RX-7's sales, especially given the fact that the sportscar market had shrunk worldwide.

Interior

Work on the interior was carried out solely in Hiroshima in an effort to both cut manufacturing costs and give the cockpit a higher quality feel. To quote the press release handed out at the Tokyo Show: 'With almost identical interior dimensions to the first generation, the new Roadster offers comfortably close interior space, enhancing the feeling of oneness between car and driver.

'The design of the T-shaped instrument panel is inherited from the first generation. The centre console wraps around both driver and passenger thanks to the low seat position. All the individual round gauges are gathered in a simple semi-circle cluster. The six-speed manual transmission model features a unique tachometer and speedmeter with needles pointing at the six o'clock start position. The steering wheel is a jointly-developed Nardi small-diameter three-spoke type with Supplemental Restraint System (SRS) airbags.

Three of the many design proposals put forward for the M2 interior.

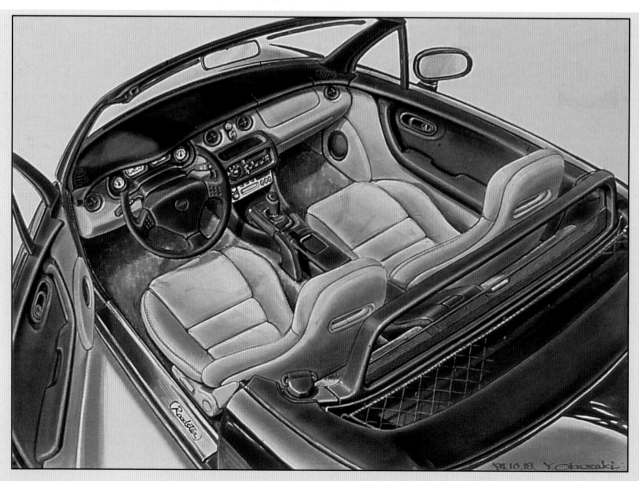

The development of the interior. Like the body, the basic concept was decided on at quite an early stage, with just detailing to be settled on as the design progressed.

The high-back bucket-type seats are superior in holding capability.

'Enlarged storage space in the door pockets and the centre console box provide greater overall storage capacity and dual cup holders in the rear console box add practicality. The Roadster's exclusive audio system, designed in co-operation with Bose, creates a stereo environment even during open driving. The speakers' thin and lightweight construction also contributes to decreased overall vehicle weight without sacrificing performance.'

The main difference was the more integrated look of the centre console, with the centre vents becoming part of the main fascia. Although the instrument layout was much the same, the odometer was now a digital readout. The 1.6 and 1.8 had different speedos and tachometers on the home market, with the smaller-engined model's needles starting from the tradi-tional eight o'clock position, as did all cars destined for export.

Finishing touches

Kijima said that although looks were important, it was driving sensation that should be consid-ered the number one priority. Chassis testing was carried out by Masashi Oda on the second batch of mules (completed in mid-1986) and S1 prototypes, with testing as a whole overseen by Takashi Takeshita, Vice-Chief of the

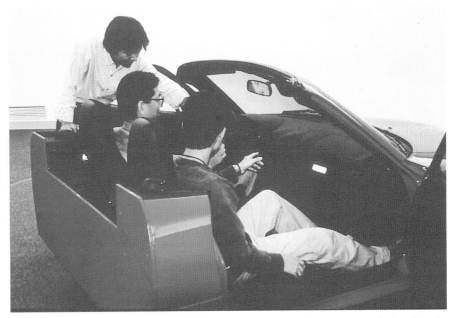

Once a design was accepted, interior styling bucks were made to check ergonomics and the general "feel" of the cockpit.

Although only 5mm wider in reality, the new car looked far wider and lower visually. As Martin Leach, the MD in charge of Product Planning, Design & Programs, said: 'It's got more presence.' Clinics had been held in both America and Japan, the car's biggest markets.

Interior of the new model. Note the 'Windblocker' behind the seats, designed to stop drafts. The hardtop anchorage points on the rear deck were carried over from the previous model.

Top right: While the original 1600 looked very basic in the luggage area, the first 1800 had a well-trimmed boot. The second generation model's luggage compartment was also carpeted, but the capacity had increased slightly to 6.1 cubic feet. However, with the spare wheel and battery moving below the boot floor, the space provided was more useful.

Bottom right: A rear view of the second generation car. Note the new lighting arrangement (this being a Japanese specification vehicle, it is equipped with twin reversing lights - one in each cluster).

American advertising showing the all-new 1999 model year Miata. The American press release stated: 'It lifts your spirit and renews your soul.' The US Press launch was held on Big Island, Hawaii, incidentally.

We didn't just rekindle an old flame.
We threw gasoline on it.

The all-new '99 Miata

Visit us at www.mazdausa.com or call 1-800-639-1000.

Production at Hiro-shima. Note the winged Mazda symbol (on the nose and it also appeared on the bootlid), said to represent 'Mazda spreading its wings as it soars into the future.'

A left-hand drive model fresh from the production line and undergoing a final series of checks.

Experimental Department.

Vehicle development took place all over the world, mainly on mock-ups using the first generation body. It is interesting to note that Oda was at first against the six-speed gearbox in the prototype stages but nonetheless it was eventually perfected.

Although Mazda insisted on one-handed operation of the hood (soft top), in reality the material used in the old rear window meant it needed to be unzipped before the lid was dropped to avoid damaging it. The new model's glass rear screen was a vast improvement as one could happily unclip the catches and let the hood fall backwards without worry. Despite the heavier glass screen, the hood as a whole was actually around 1kg lighter than its predecessor.

The added strength of the new body made the cockpit brace bar unnecessary, but there was another interesting feature behind the seats - a wind blocker (or anti-draft panel), as found on the RX-7 Cabriolet. Mazda's unique 'Windblocker is incorporated behind the seats to reduce wind turbulence entering the leg room from behind during open driving. The result is an improved heater which enhances comfort during open winter driving.'

In its lightest home market form, the new Roadster weighed in at 1000kg. This meant a 60kg increase compared to the original, but it was only 20kg more than the basic 1.8-litre Series II model. Kijima was justifiably proud of this achievement, reiterating that a light package was absolutely crucial.

The pilot build took place in Hiroshima, with these earliest cars once again having the S1 designation; the run was completed in January 1997. Thanks to the use of DPA (Digital Pre-Assembly, which allows the cars to be "built" on computer before tackling the real thing), very little rectification was needed before the car started production.

Eager anticipation

By the end of 1996 speculation about the MX-5 was rife. *Complete Car* magazine in the UK noted in September: 'Mazda's MX-5 will be in for a facelift by the end of next year, with the now old-fashioned pop-up lights being dropped. The revamp will be subtle ... but further ahead Mazda may also consider a more muscular, performance version of the car as an image-booster.'

As early as July 1997, several British magazines were carrying details of the new MX-5 after somebody put a Mazda promotional video on the Internet. The new headlight arrangement was obvious from the various spy shots that were published after the leak, but much to Mazda's dismay, virtually everyone knew the full details of the MX-5's replacement months before the planned launch at the 1997 Tokyo Show.

Although specifications were fairly clear by now, no-one outside the company knew how the car would drive. It was felt that Mazda was not going to let the new car fall below the standard the first generation model had set, but it would be reassuring to know for sure.

Writing for *Road & Track* in September 1997, Thos. L. Bryant teased enthusiasts with the following statement: 'In the spring, Mazda Motors of America's Vice-President of Public Affairs, Jay Amestoy, suggested that a small group of us should go to Japan to meet with the people designing and engineering the upcoming new Miata ... I am sworn to secrecy, but I will allow as how the new version is sure to please.'

The scene was set ...

Despite various leaks threatening to spoil the build-up, the new car's official launch at the 32nd Tokyo Show was still a big event for the world's media. The press conference was held on October 22, three days before the doors at Makuhari Messe opened to the public.

In the highlights booklet handed out at the Tokyo Show, the new Mazda Roadster (the Eunos name had been dropped), was given top billing in the Mazda section: 'The all-new Roadster makes its world debut at the Tokyo Motor Show. This superb car embodies the enduring appeal of authentic lightweight sportscars.

'The new Roadster employs a lightweight, compact and highly-rigid two-seater open body. Its exterior features modern sportscar styling carried over from the original Roadster model. Under the hood, Mazda offers a choice of either a 1.8-litre or 1.6-litre engine with enhanced power. These engines work in harmony with the car's advanced chassis to improve driving feel, responsive handling and smooth ride.

'The 1.8-litre-engined model comes with a close-ratio six-speed manual transmission. The new Roadster also features the highly-rigid MAGMA safety body.'

Mazda had two of the new Roadsters on display - a gold-coloured model (a stunning shade that was used extensively in the early publicity shots from around the time of the launch) and one finished in a tasteful dark green.

However, apart from the new MX-5s and a solitary RX-7, the theme of the Mazda stand very much reflected the fashions of the

The launch of the second generation Mazda Roadster at the 1997 Tokyo Show. This photograph was taken by the author on the first press day.

Mazda actually had two of the new Roadsters on display at the 1997 Tokyo Show - the gold-coloured model on the rotating stand and this top-of-the-range VS in Grey Green Mica.

The green Roadster at the 1997 Tokyo Show was mounted high up in the centre of the Mazda stand. The coachwork colour and tan interior show it to be a 1.8-litre VS model.

MIATA MX-5 EUNOS

time, with MPVs and estate cars dominating. No-one could blame the management, though, as this was the strongest sector of the market in Japan as the millennium loomed, while sportscars were in danger of becoming a dying breed. Perhaps this was another reason Mazda didn't go too crazy with a brand new design, it being prudent to stick with a proven winner.

The press release issued at the show (but dated 15 October) read as follows: 'Defined as a new vehicle to be marketed in the future, the all-new Mazda Roadster will be exhibited. Since its world debut in 1989, the first generation Mazda Roadster has been [widely] touted as the best two-seater lightweight roadster in the world. The new Roadster inherits virtues of the first generation and balances all the strong points of top-down driving fun with superb sportscar performance and incomparable styling.' It also listed the following nine points:

1) The dimensions of the new Mazda Roadster are 3955mm in overall length, 1680mm in overall width, 1235mm in overall height and 2265mm in wheelbase. Only the overall width is 5mm greater than its predecessor.

2) The basic layout maintains the front-engine rear-drive layout achieving an ideal front and rear weight distribution. The engine is mounted mid-ship behind the axle [*i.e.* quite far back in the engine bay].

3) Carrying on the design motif recognizable at a glance as the Roadster, the new Roadster is designed to offer sportier, aggressive and dynamic styling in a

Despite having the MS-X, MV-X and SW-X concept cars at the Tokyo Show, it was the new Roadster that made the cover of Mazda's event brochure.

First Japanese brochure for the 2nd generation Roadster. The gold colour (known by different names around the world) was used extensively in build-up publicity and launch material.

three-dimensional form.

4) Either 1.8-litre or 1.6-litre in-line four-cylinder dohc 16v engines are available. With refinement of the intake and exhaust systems, both engines have improved output and torque, enhanced revving characteristics and greater acceleration response.

5) The 1.8-litre-engined model features a newly-developed six-speed manual transmission which optimizes engine speed and acceleration characteristics at high revs.

6) The double-wishbone suspension at the front and rear is further enhanced. Through reviewing the geometry and fine tuning, the driving stability of the new Roadster was refined for more fun driving.

7) By incorporating a glass window with defoggers the view through the rear window was greatly improved. By dropping the zipper around the vinyl rear window open and close operations were eased, while overall weight of the softtop was reduced.

8) The highly rigid and safe body Mazda Advanced Impact Distribution and Absorption System achieves enhanced collision safety (also known as MAGMA or Mazda Geometric Motion Absorption). The well-managed body torsion and vibration as a result of increase in the body rigidity contribute to the superb driving stability of the new Roadster.

9) In addition to the driver's and passenger's SRS (Supplemental Restraint System) airbags, the

The brochure handed out at the Tokyo Show described all the salient points of the new Roadster. The Mazda stand had both the ubiquitous gold-coloured example and another finished in dark green (known as Grey Green Metallic in Japan).

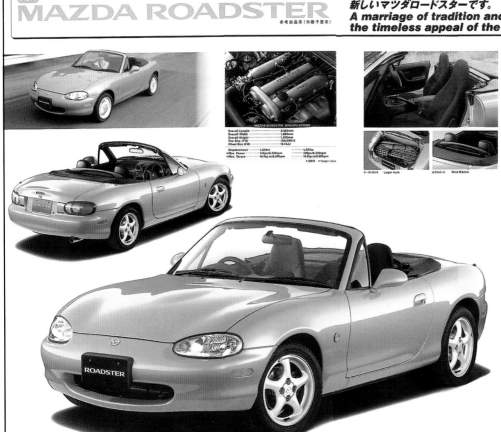

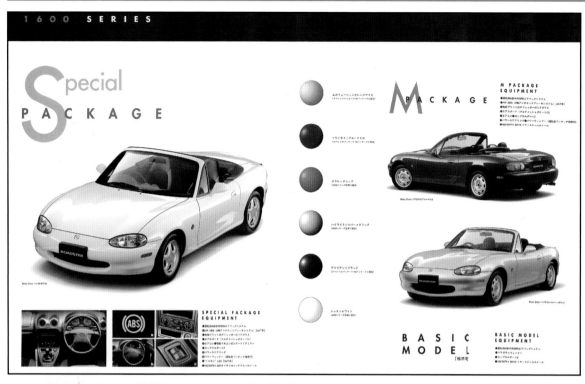

The Japanese 1600 range as seen in the first catalogue released for the new model.

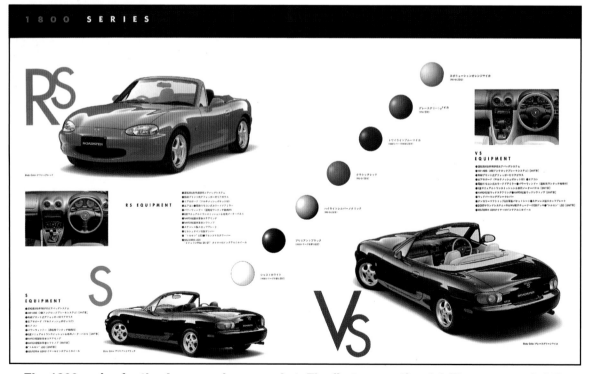

The 1800 series for the Japanese home market. The first generation 1.6-litre cars carried the NA6CE chassis designation, whereas 1.8-litre models were identified by the NA8C prefix. For the second generation, the smaller-engined car carried the NB6C code, while the 1.8-litre vehicles were known by the NB8C chassis number.

A series of four advertisements for the new Roadster. Each describes a notable feature, such as the MAGMA body, six-speed transmission, double-wishbone suspension all-round and the traditional FR layout.

seatbelts are equipped with an automatic tension function that regulates tension force against a certain level of impact with the occupants.

Of course, Mazda no longer had the convertible market to itself, and more cars were joining the MX-5 all the time. Announced at the 1997 Tokyo Show alongside the new car from Hiroshima, the Toyota MR-S was an indirect replacement for the MR2, designed to compete head-on with the MX-5. Due to go into production in 1999, the new Toyota should give an interesting comparison test with the Mazda Roadster. Another debutante at Makuhari Messe was the Suzuki C2 - a lightweight open car powered by a 250bhp, 1.6-litre V8. The future is definitely going to be interesting ...

The home market

As usual, the Japanese market had an extensive line-up of models. The 1.6-litre range included a basic five-speed model, the M Package and Special Package. Both these latter versions could be bought with a five-speed manual gearbox or a four-speed automatic transmission. ABS brakes came as standard with the automatic models and were an option on the manual M Package and Special Package cars. All 1.6s came with Mazda's own four-spoke steering wheel.

As for the 1.8-litre car, this was available in three different specifications - the S, RS and VS. These came with a six-speed manual gearbox but the four-speed automatic transmission was available on the S and VS. An ABS

braking system was included in the price on all automatic 1.8-litre cars and an option on each of the manual models.

All 1.8 models came with a Nardi three-spoke steering wheel and the S and RS had a leather-wrapped rim; the VS wheel was wood rimmed with matching gearknob and handbrake lever handle. Polished treadplates were standard on the RS and VS, and the latter also came with a CD player straight from the factory.

Five-spoke alloy wheels came as standard on the 1.6-litre Special Package and the three 1.8-litre grades, although the sizes were different - 185/60 HR14 tyres mounted on 6J x 14 rims was the norm, but the RS came with 195/50 VR15 tyres and 6J x 15 alloys; the basic 1.6 and M Package had 185/60 tyres on 5.5J x 14 pressed steel wheels. Likewise, a Torsen limited-slip differential came with the same range of vehicles, but only when specified in manual guise. Overall weights ranged from 1000 to 1060kg, incidentally.

Prices started at 1,819,000 yen for the basic 1.6-litre model and rose to 2,665,000 yen for the top VS models. The RS was slightly cheaper than the equivalent VS model as the VS had a higher level of trim. Sales started in January 1998 through both Mazda and Anfini dealerships - the Eunos sales channel no longer existed.

Standard exterior colours on the 1.6-litre cars included Classic Red, Highlight Silver Metallic and Chaste White. By opting for the Special Package or M Package, three more options became available: Evolution Orange Mica,

Twilight Blue Mica, and Brilliant Black. In all cases, trim was finished in black.

Twilight Blue Mica, Brilliant Black and Chaste White could be specified on all 1.8-litre models. The RS and S grades were also available in Evolution Orange Mica (the gold shade that Mazda used in most of its publicity material), Classic Red and High-light Silver Metallic, while the VS was offered in Grey Green Mica. Again, interior trim was in black except for the VS which came with tan leather trim and tan-coloured hood.

The second generation Stateside

The 1998 Detroit Show (which opened on 10 January) saw the official American launch of the second generation Miata (although it had appeared at Los Angeles a week before), tagged as a 1999 Model Year car (there would be no 1998 Model Year vehicles). Richard Beattie, President of Mazda North America, said: 'The weather outside may be cold and dreary, but with the introduction of our new Miata, things are heating up at Mazda. As good as the original Miata was, this new 1999 Miata is better in every single way. We fully expect it to remain the best-selling two-seat roadster on the planet.'

The press release said: 'The car that almost single-handedly revived the two-seat open roadster market around the world arrived in Detroit today as Mazda executives unveiled the all-new 1999 Miata at the 1998 North American International Auto Show. The new Miata, which features a more powerful engine, dramatically restyled body, redesigned interior and improved handling, goes on sale in Mazda dealerships early in 1998.

'The new 1999 Mazda Miata features a more powerful 140hp 1.8-litre dohc four-cylinder engine, improved four-wheel double-wishbone suspension, more aggressively styled body and a redesigned interior. The body of the new Miata is more rigid for improved handling, yet it weighs the same as its predecessor. The easy-to-use folding top is even easier to operate and now uses a glass rear window with built-in defroster, a feature not found on several convertibles costing much more.

'The new Mazda Miata may not be on sale yet, but the editors of *Car & Driver* magazine are already hailing it as one of the "10 Best Cars" in the publication's January 1998 issue. This is nothing new for the Miata - the original car won several awards and accolades before it went on sale as well.

'Since its introduction in 1989, Mazda has sold more than 450,000 Miatas worldwide, with more than half of that total coming to North America. The Miata is the best-selling two-seat roadster in the world. In addition, the Mazda Miata is a champion on the track, earning several SCCA Class championships.'

As they had with the previous generation car, Mazda's marketing people bombarded journalists with press releases about the new car in a bid to get that extra column inch, but the underlying message was usually the same: 'Despite all of the

One of the photographs in the Detroit Show press release. The caption reads: 'The 1999 Miata is proof that the sequel can be better than the original. Featuring a dramatically restyled body, improved handling, a glass rear window with defroster and an increase in horsepower to 140, the all-new Miata is ready to continue its reign as the best-selling two-seat roadster in the world.' The car features the 15 inch alloys that come as part of the Leather Package.

American advertising from early 1998. Note the air dam at the front, meaning the car used in the picture was fitted with the Sports Package.

A rear view of the 1999 Miata for the American market. Note the optional five-spoke alloy wheels - these are the 14 inch versions, although the 15 inch items look very similar.

The 1.8-litre BP-ZE (RS) engine that powers the US range - the 1.6 unit is not listed in America. Rated at 140bhp in most States, cars for California, New York, Massachusetts and Connecticut lost 2bhp due to tighter emissions regulations.

Interior of the standard Miata showing the Nardi steering wheel supplied as part of the Touring Package. Again, American cars have to do without the option of a wood rimmed wheel.

changes to the 1999 Mazda Miata, it remains true to its original concept - a lightweight, affordable, two-seat roadster that delivers the pure enjoyment of wind-in-the-hair driving. It lifts your spirit and renews your soul.'

America had only the 1.8-litre car. With a 9.5:1 compression ratio,

it was rated at 140bhp at 6500rpm (or 138bhp in California), and had a maximum torque output of 119lb/ft at 5500rpm (vehicles for California developed 2lb/ft less but at a more useful 5000rpm).

The base model had a five-speed manual gearbox, rack-and-pinion non-assisted steering and

185/60 HR14 tyres mounted on 5.5J x 14 pressed steel wheels. All cars came with dual airbags as standard and - amazingly - a combined stereo radio/CD player with a digital clock. Basic options included air conditioning, power steering, fog lights and bright wheel trim rings. There were now

The Leather Package's stylish interior. Seat facings are trimmed in tan leather and the rest is finished in a matching vinyl. The passenger airbag can actually be de-activated to allow a child seat to be used.

The Miata where it belongs - on the road giving fun.

five option packages to choose from:

Touring Package: This added power-assisted steering, 6J x 14 alloy wheels, power windows and mirrors and a Nardi three-spoke leather-rimmed steering wheel. Automatic transmission became an option with this package.

Popular Equipment Package: This included the items in the Touring Package, plus a Torsen lsd (on manual cars), cruise control, power door locks, an upgraded sound system, electric aerial and the wind blocker. ABS brakes became an option if the Bose stereo system was bought at the same time.

Leather Package: Based on the Popular Equipment Package but with the added bonus of a tan leather interior and tan-coloured hood, 195/50 VR15 Michelin Pilot SX GT tyres mounted on 6J x 15 alloys, plus the high-powered Bose stereo radio/cassette/CD unit with top quality speakers. ABS brakes were optional.

Sports Package: This came with manual cars only and included a Torsen limited-slip differential, 15 inch alloys with the 195/50 tyres, a three-spoke Nardi leather-rimmed steering wheel, an uprated suspension (including Bilstein shock absorbers), a front strut tower brace, front air dam and rear spoiler.

Appearance Package: The Appearance Package was not available with the Sports Package, but included a front air dam, side skirts, a rear spoiler, rear mudflaps and fog lights.

Standard colours included White, Brilliant Black, Classic Red, Twilight Blue Mica, Highlight

One of the pictures that came with the Geneva Show press pack. Mazda gave almost as much attention to the 626 and various concept cars that had made their debut almost five months earlier in Tokyo as it did to the MX-5.

Silver Metallic and Emerald Mica. Trim was in black cloth, or tan leather, although the latter was not available with the Sports Package. Prices started at $19,770.

The new car in Europe

The second generation MX-5 made its European debut at the 1998 Geneva Show held from 5 to 15 March. In his opening statement at the Swiss event, James E. Miller said: 'I am delighted to welcome you to the Geneva Motor Show for the first time as President of the Mazda Motor Corporation. Mazda has earned an excellent reputation for superior design and engineering capabilities - a reputation that reflects its attention to form, functionality and advanced

technology, as well as its emphasis on creativity and craftsmanship.

'Today Mazda exhibits automobiles that exemplify our new approach based on this long-standing tradition: the all-new MX-5, the new 626 Station Wagon and the Demio Concept along with the MV-X and SW-X concept cars. The new MX-5 will be marketed in Europe from April. Redesign features heighten response and power for truly fun sportscar driving, yet keep the feeling of oneness between car and driver that MX-5 users have come to expect and love. We hope you will feel the strength of our enthusiasm for the future of automobiles through the cars and technology you will see at this show.'

The press pack highlighted the following points -

Compact, Fun-to-Drive Package

The optimum product package, balanced for driving pleasure. Mazda made extra efforts to minimize the vehicle weight of the new MX-5. Decreasing both front and rear overhang weight and placing all the mass as close to the vehicle centre as possible, enabled the new MX-5 to achieve excellent yaw inertia moment and ideal weight distribution.

More Sporty Look and Feel

The body is attractive from all angles and retains the MX-5's distinctive design motif. Its sporty

A shot of the MX-5 in action, but this is a UK-spec 1.8iS. Sales in the UK started on 25 April.

A British 1.6i. This car is fitted with 14 inch alloys supplied as a £440 option through dealerships. The 1.6i was launched at a list price of £15,520.

Interior of the MX-5 1.8iS with Nardi three-spoke steering wheel. The wind blocker can clearly be seen behind the seats.

The 1.8iS was the UK's top model, priced at £18,775. It came with 6J x 15 alloys and a host of extras as standard, but the detachable hardtop was a pricey £1475 option.

A rear view of the European (lhd) spec MX-5. This picture shows the softtop - and therefore the new glass rear window - fully erected, along with the latest rear light design which eliminates the need for a separate fog light.

look is enhanced by lines that stress the wide and low form. Inside, the cockpit is simple and more functional.

Excellent Driving Pleasure

The new MX-5 offers sharply enhanced driving performance when compared with the original MX-5, thanks to the powerful 1.8-litre and 1.6-litre in-line four-cylinder dohc 16v engine and excellent driving stability, made possible by a highly rigid body and chassis. The five-speed manual transmission further enhances the fun of sports driving.

Superb Safety Features

The new Mazda MX-5 offers excellent active safety features to help prevent accidents, and outstanding passive safety features to help protect the driver and the passenger in the event of an accident.

Improved Functionality for Daily Use

The new MX-5 delivers enhanced

practicality with more convenient and comfort-enhancing functions and features.

The UK press launch was held on the French Riviera, with the car going on sale to the public from the end of April. Special music, *The Song of the Swift* by John Harle, was played at the dealerships and tape cassettes given away in boxes finished in the same gold colour as seen on the new MX-5. In years to come these will doubtless be collectors' items!

The UK press release stated: 'The new Mazda MX-5 offers enhanced performance and excellent handling and stability. The 0-62mph acceleration time for the 1.6-litre is now just 9.7 seconds, a reduction of 0.9 seconds. The 1.8-litre reaches 0-62mph in 8.0 seconds, down 0.7 seconds from the previous car. Top speed for the 1.6-litre is now 118mph (up 9mph) and 127mph (up 4mph) for the 1.8-litre.

'The 1.6-litre has had power increased by 20bhp (from 90bhp to 110bhp). The 1.8-litre is up 9bhp (from 131bhp to 140bhp). Output and torque for both engines have been improved through enhancements to the intake and exhaust systems, resulting in smooth engine revving from low to high speeds and responsive acceleration.'

All of the new MX-5s were sold with powered-steering, an immobiliser and driver and passenger airbags as standard; steel 5.5J x 14 tyres were the norm, fitted with 185/60 HR14 tyres. The 1.8-litre model added electric windows and a wind blocker to the basic specification, while the 1.8iS also came with 195/50 VR15 tyres mounted on 6J x 15 alloys and a number of other more upmarket touches - ABS braking, a Torsen lsd, electrically-adjusted door mirrors, a Nardi leather-rimmed steering wheel, power door locks, stereo radio/cassette with electric aerial, mudflaps and stainless treadplates.

In Britain, the 1.6i was listed at £15,520 on the road (almost £1000 more than its predecessor, or about the price of the old 1.8i); the new 1.8i was priced at £16,650, whilst the 1.8iS price was little changed at £18,775. Major options included air conditioning, a detachable hardtop, front fog lamps and a rear spoiler. The wind blocker, alloy wheels, stainless treadplates and front and rear mudflaps were also made available to upgrade cheaper models.

Standard colours included Classic Red, Classic Black, Racing Silver Metallic, Racing Blue Mica, Racing Green Mica and Racing Bronze Mica, although metallic and mica shades added £250 to the price of the car. Trim was usually a black cloth, but leather could be specified as a £923 option, colour choices being black, light grey, anthracite, tan, taupe and mist.

It is interesting to note that automatic transmission was not listed anywhere in Europe. Some European mainland countries such as Italy got the 15 inch alloy wheels as standard on both the 1.6 and 1.8-litre models, although the ABS braking system, Torsen limited-slip differential, and Nardi steering wheel were reserved for the larger-engined car.

Switzerland had two 1.6-litre grades (the 1.6 Youngster and 1.6 SE Youngster), and one 1.8 - the 1.8 Youngster. The basic 1.6 came with steel wheels and standard brakes, but the other grades had 15 inch alloys and ABS as standard. Only the 1.8 was fitted with the Torsen lsd, however. Overall weights on European cars ranged from 1015kg for the basic 1.6 to 1047kg for the UK spec 1.8iS.

Mazdaspeed

As Mazda's representative in the field of motorsport and the factory's outlet for works tuning parts, it's not surprising that Mazdaspeed was first to offer aerodynamic body kits and tuning components. In a news release dated 26 February, the Touring Kit A-Spec was announced: 'Mazdaspeed Co. Ltd is proud to announce that the Touring Kit A-Spec for the new Roadster (NB8C/NB6C) is now under development and will be available through its Sport Factory, other nationwide Mazda group dealers and retailers from 26 February 1998.

'Development of the Touring Kit A-Spec has been made on the orthodox and evolutionary concept focusing on the aerodynamic and suspension parts to withdraw maximum onroad potential. A special feature of the tuning parts is the overall three-dimensional body design with which wind tunnel tests showed a positive improvement to the Cd [the air resistance factor] and Cl [the lift factor] readings. In addition, the front spoiler is that of the first generation Air Scoop design reducing air resistance. Further-

NEW ROADSTER

TOURING KIT A-spec.

スポーツカーの
正統なる進化。

新型ロードスター用
「ツーリングキット A-スペック」
新発売！

MAZDASPEED

nitrogen treatment has been carried out on the flywheel surface, making this product a sufficiently hard and durable item.

'Moreover, suspension parts, sports sound muffler, exhaust manifold, roll bar, sports driving meters [white-faced gauges], high volt silicone leads and the brake line set are presently undergoing development and will be available from April.

'Among the selections of Touring kit devised for public roads is the Touring Kit A-Spec. Parts used exclusively for competition make up the Sports Kit and each part can be purchased separately to suit the needs and budget of the buyer.'

Prices ranged from 35,000 yen for the headlight finishers to 58,000 yen for a rear spoiler or the side skirts. The body kit was completed by the front spoiler and rear skirt, each priced at 48,000 yen. Mazdaspeed seats ranged from 64,000 to 88,000 yen.

Mechanical components for the 1.8-litre car included the limited-slip differential at 75,000 yen and the front pad set at 15,000 yen (2000 yen more than for the rear set). For both power units, 48,000 yen would buy the lightened flywheel, while the clutch set was 54,000 yen on the 1.8, or 52,000 on the 1.6-litre. Other prices had not been released at the time.

Initial press reaction

In America *Motor Trend* was very quick to cover the new model, claiming that 'Although the second generation of this petite two-seater rolls onto the scene next spring with a new look and new level of

more, the headlight finisher has been designed to provide a smooth look with a strong outline definition. Moreover, the three-dimensional shaped side skirt allows the air flow to channel smoothly by the body side. All other aero-parts, namely the rear wing and rear skirt, have undergone wind tunnel tests to find their optimum setting to increase the aerodynamic effect.

'Optional parts designed for the new Roadster (MX-5) include the newly-designed air filter. This adopts three special layered Welten Sponges which in tests showed a suction restriction of 20 per cent, contributing to better fuel economy and accelerator response. Also, [for the 1.8-litre car, there is a] limited-slip differential which has been designed for better traction for both wheels, enabling controlled and effective cornering.

'An additional item [for the 1.8-litre model] is the asbestos-free brake set designed for durability and controllability. The clutch set has been designed to transmit high power from the engine to the drivetrain. Furthermore, a lighter flywheel is available, enabling a quick engine response without engine stall or difficult clutch operation. A shaving process of the chrome-molybdenum and the ion-

Mazdaspeed's Touring Kit A-Spec for the new Roadster announced in February 1998, a month after sales of the second generation model began in Japan.

sophistication, remaining fully intact are all the wonderful traits that made the original car fun to drive and easy to own.' This view was echoed in *Road & Track*, the sub-heading of its April 1998 test reading: 'The same basic formula taken to new heights.'

Thos. L. Bryant introduced the car to Australian readers in *Wheels* magazine, and had this to say: 'The tail of the MX-5 proto-type wiggled just a little as I went through a series of esses at the Miyoshi proving ground. The message from the car was polite but firm: "You're going too fast for these conditions." As I eased off and the all-new MX-5 settled itself, a grin spread across my face. I've loved the MX-5 since it was introduced in 1989, but this new one is markedly improved.'

Writing for the popular British *Top Gear* magazine in February 1998, Yasushi Ishiwatari

noted: 'Though it's not exactly a quantum leap in styling from the old MX-5, there's more to be enthusiastic about than you'd think; it really does feel more like a new car than anyone would imagine from looking at it ... It hasn't lost any of the charm of its predecessor. The good points have been further improved, and they've fixed many of the niggly and irritating problems.'

The same journal carried out a comparison test between the MX-5 1.8iS, MGF and Fiat Barchetta. Although opinion was that the new car was not as much fun as the original, and that it had lost some of its character, the Mazda still came out on top.

In a similar test, *Car* thought it was a clear-cut decision in favour of the car from Hiroshima, and *Autocar* (who added a BMW Z3 into the equation) was also wooed by the appeal of the MX-5.

In its verdict on the new 1.8-litre MX-5, *Autocar* stated in another article: 'Much improved chassis; better quality interior materials make the cabin more classy. Mazda's jewel finely polished.'

As you will have gathered, almost all of the early road tests were complimentary and Mazda was often praised for not making changes for the sake of it. The Japanese *Motor Magazine* summed up the mood perfectly: 'The new car is the next level up from the first generation Eunos Roadster. The looks have changed, but the soul remains the same.'

After an uncertain start to life, the MX-5 went on to take the world by storm. If initial reactions are anything to go by, the future looks set to be every bit as good as the past has been for Mazda's LWS ...

The figures below are taken from official Mazda records. The first table shows production figures and the number of cars exported in each year; running totals for both are added in. Given the short production life, and state of the world economy and sports car sales in general, these figures are very impressive. The second table breaks down sales in the main markets, i.e. Japan, the USA, Canada, Europe (including the UK) and Australia.

Year	Annual Production	Cumulative Production	Annual Exports	Cumulative Exports
1988	12	12	0	0
1989	45,266	45,278	34,021	34,021
1990	95,640	140,918	67,400	101,421
1991	63,434	204,352	40,729	142,150
1992	52,712	257,064	34,096	176,246
1993	44,743	301,807	27,909	204,155
1994	39,623	341,430	29,079	233,234
1995	31,886	373,316	27,648	260,882
1996	33,610	406,926	29,231	290,113
1997	27,037	433,963	22,856	312,969

Year	Japanese Sales	American Sales	Canadian Sales	European Sales	Australian Sales
1988	0	0	0	0	0
1989	9307	23,052	2827	0	621
1990	25,226	35,944	3906	9267	1446
1991	22,594	31,240	2956	14,050	746
1992	18,657	24,964	2277	6631	502
1993	16,789	21,588	1501	4824	453
1994	10,830	21,400	1173	5019	404
1995	7178	20,174	934	7716	196
1996	4413	18,408	558	9585	241
Totals	114,994	196,770	16,132	57,092	4609

MIATA
MX-5
EUNOS

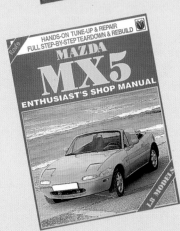

The Mazda Motor Corporation, its
subsidiaries and products are
mentioned throughout the book.